It Takes a Town to Raise an Orphan

It Takes a Town to Raise an Orphan

Jimmy Brown the Orphan Boy, Volume 2

JAMES BROWN

Published by JAMES BROWN, 2023.

IT TAKES A TOWN TO RAISE AN ORPHAN

First edition. December 18, 2023.

Copyright © 2023 JAMES BROWN.

ISBN: 979-8227292223

Written by JAMES BROWN.

Also by JAMES BROWN

Jimmy Brown the Orphan Boy
It Takes a Town to Raise an Orphan

Standalone
An Orphan's Goodbyes: A Memoir

Watch for more at https://jimmybrownclub.com.

Table of Contents

IT TAKES A TOWN TO RAISE AN ORPHAN

James Brown

IT TAKES A TOWN TO RAISE AN ORPHAN

Disclaimer: I have tried to recreate events, locales, and conversations from my memories of them. To protect privacy, in some instances I have changed the names of individuals and places. I may have changed some identifying characteristics and details, such as physical properties, occupations, and places of residence.

Although the author has made every effort to ensure that the information in this book was correct at the time of publication, the author does not assume and hereby disclaims any liability to any party for any loss, damage, or disruption caused by errors or omissions, whether such errors or omissions result from negligence, accident, or any other cause.

Dedication

To all the people who worked in the orphanage where I grew up until I was twelve years old, and to my best friend, Bobby Broberg.

Acknowledgments

Writing this book brought back a lot of memories of what it was like to be part of a community that cares for their youth. As I cherished the thoughts of my young life, I knew I wanted to leave a legacy for my family and friends.

I am grateful for Candace Sinclair who gave me guidance and encouragement to put those years into a story of how a town contributes to one person's beliefs.

I especially want to thank my wife, Charlotte Moncato, for all the years of growing and guidance, for she was the angel who came into my life.

Table of Contents

Chapter One
Where Are They Taking Me?

Twelve-year-old Jimmy Brown was excited to return to the orphanage after his summer break living with Grandpa and Aunt Thelma. As an orphan boy, Jimmy was happy they had welcomed him into their home for eight years of summer vacations from school. Many children in the orphanage weren't as fortunate, since they didn't have any family to spend their summers with, but they did have each other.

Earlier that morning, Uncle Frank Culver from Wisconsin came to assist Grandpa with taking Jimmy back to the orphanage. They loaded up Jimmy's clothes into a suitcase, and the three of them drove forty miles from Lexington, Nebraska to the orphanage in Holdrege, Nebraska.

As soon as the car came to a halt in front of the orphanage where Jimmy had lived since he was three years old, he jumped out and ran up the steps of the home. Within seconds, he was downstairs in the playroom with the other boys, including Stanley and Sterling, the Fastenal twins.

Stanley pulled Jimmy aside and said, "Most of the kids moved out this summer, which leaves only twenty of us boys and fifteen girls. We heard they were trying to close down the orphanage."

Jimmy said, "Let's go out in the yard and you can tell me what everyone did this summer."

Jimmy was excited to see all his old friends again and learn what they had been doing. But what he wanted to know were two things: who got into the most trouble, and how did his closest friends do with their prized cows at the 4H showing at the fairgrounds?

Jimmy was catching up with his friends and what they had done over the summer at the orphanage when the snack bell rang at 3 o'clock. All the children left the playroom to line up at the dining room door.

They always looked forward to the treats, such as an apple, an orange, or fresh-baked slices of cake, a cinnamon roll, or other baked goods.

Without warning, the door to the downstairs dining room swung open. A matron, Anna, stepped inside and hollered, "Jimmy Brown?"

"That's me," said Jimmy.

The tall lady looked at Jimmy and moved silently toward him, saying, "I'm going to escort you back upstairs to the office where your Uncle Frank and Grandpa are waiting for you."

With a puzzled look on his face, Jimmy followed her to the office. When he walked through the door, he saw Grandpa and Uncle Frank.

Uncle Frank said, "We're leaving now, Jimmy. You need to get in the car with me and your Grandpa."

Jimmy asked, "Why? We just got here. I don't understand. I haven't even put my clothes away. I need to say goodbye to my friends. When are we coming back? Why are we leaving, Grandpa?"

Grandpa gently took hold of Jimmy's hand as they walked down the twenty-five wide steps that led to the front door of the orphanage.

"Let's just get in the car, Jimmy. Then we'll talk," Grandpa said in a matter-of-fact tone of voice.

With a look of panic and confusion on Jimmy's face, he was obedient and followed Grandpa and Uncle Frank to the car. When he opened up the back door, he saw his suitcase sitting on the seat. He crawled inside the car, reluctantly, and then popped the latches open on his suitcase. He saw that all his clothes were inside. His sad look needed no words.

As Uncle Frank drove the car down the long driveway heading to the highway, Grandpa turned to Jimmy in the back seat.

Grandpa said, "They have decided to close the orphanage next month. Given all our options on where you should go, the superintendent thought you should come and live with me, because you have a lot of family members in the area to help me take care of you. Now let's just have a peaceful ride back to town. When we get there and have a little meal and some refreshments, your Uncle Frank and I will tell you the whole story."

With a shocked look on his face and knowing it wasn't the time to start asking more questions, Jimmy slumped back into the seat and stared out the window as the countryside whizzed by.

Once they arrived back at Grandpa's house, Grandpa made sandwiches and Uncle Frank made iced tea. Grandpa pulled up another chair at the table for Uncle Frank.

"Sit down, Jimmy boy," Grandpa said, "and we'll tell you everything that happened."

Jimmy sat at his place at the white, flowered, oil-cloth-covered table in the dining room.

Uncle Frank said, "You're ready to start junior high school. Your grandpa and I believe you're old enough and mature enough to hear the truth about what really happened today."

Jimmy listened intently.

Grandpa was the first to speak. "The superintendent gave me a choice. He told me the state was closing all the children's orphanages. They would place all orphan children into foster homes if they were still there when the orphanage closed next month. I was being asked to make a decision whether I should let them put you in a foster home, put you up for adoption, or have you come live with me or another relative."

Jimmy protested, "But Grandpa you're so old. You're seventy-eight, aren't you? And you have no money except retirement, right? How can you afford to take care of me? I have needs. Who is going to cook for me and do my laundry? Where will I go to school for seventh grade?"

Grandpa knew that none of his children would take Jimmy in to live with them. And putting the young blond-haired boy up for adoption was more than Grandpa thought his heart could tolerate.

Grandpa said, "If I took one of those other options, then I might never see you again. If I put you in a foster home, I wouldn't know where you were or how you were being treated."

Uncle Frank could sense Grandpa's tenseness, and his slowness to answer made the silence and the air feel thick. Jimmy deserved answers.

Uncle Frank looked Jimmy straight in the eye. "Your grandpa and I don't think you'd like being moved from foster home to foster home, and we couldn't bear in our hearts to put you up for adoption. Most families want younger children. We didn't want you to feel abandoned. And although most of your other relatives are not financially able to take you into their homes, we felt it was best for you to live here. Somehow with the help of God we will do just fine."

Jimmy stopped eating his sandwich, took a gulp of iced tea and looked back at Uncle Frank.

"I heard you and Aunt Thelma saying that Grandpa wouldn't be around a few years from now."

Grandpa and Uncle Frank exchanged glances.

Jimmy looked at Grandpa and said, "Sorry Grandpa, but that's what they said."

Grandpa put his hand on Jimmy's shoulder and looking into Jimmy's eyes, he softly said, "Jim, none of us know when the Lord will call us home. So, let's do what we can do to make this work. I know you didn't have a say in any of this, but we want what's best for you. Do you understand?"

After a long, silent pause, Jimmy sat up a little straighter in his chair and announced, "I'm going to get through this with you, Grandpa. Thank you for deciding to keep me with you. I know I wouldn't have liked living in a bunch of foster homes. And I sure wouldn't want someone to adopt me. I'd miss you and everyone I care about."

Chapter Two
Jimmy's New Life with Grandpa Begins

That night, thirteen-year-old Jimmy laid in a goose feather bed with Grandpa, who was already asleep. Grandpa had a small red radio with jazz music playing softly. The light from the radio lit up the ceiling, which was why Jimmy couldn't sleep. He was used to all the lights being out and sleeping in pitch darkness, like in the orphanage. He felt sad knowing he'd probably never see his friends from the home again. Yet, he was happy Grandpa had chosen him and wanted to take care of him. Many orphaned kids probably didn't get that option, Jimmy thought.

As Jimmy stared up at the ceiling, he wondered how he would adjust to this new permanent living arrangement and school situation after moving to Lexington, Nebraska. He'd soon be entering a public school that was located in the local high school building on Washington Street, five blocks from downtown Lexington.

He thought back to how he had been taught in a one-room classroom from first grade to sixth grade by one teacher, Mrs. Johnson. She was employed by the Christian Home establishment along with Ms. Nelson who taught sixth to eighth grade in the next room down the hall from Mrs. Johnson's. Those classrooms were on the second floor of the three-story brick building.

Living with Grandpa Full Time

Most of the time I had to fend for myself because Grandpa would be out fishing early in the morning when I got up for school. Sometimes he would leave me some cold oatmeal or cereal out of the box. For lunch I would get home and make my own sandwiches or open a can of soup, heat it up for my lunch, and then ride my bike back to school.

Learning how to take care of myself alone with no one helping was certainly challenging, but I was soon getting good at making pancakes, pudding, and meatloaf from the recipes on the outside of boxes the products came in or the old cookbook I found in a dresser drawer. I learned to fish and how to clean the fish. I also helped prepare the chickens and made my own oatmeal in the mornings.

My clothing was washed by Aunt Thelma. She came by the house two or three times a week just to check up to see if I was getting enough to eat. Sometimes she would leave some food at the house, and sometimes she left me spending money to buy lunch at Millie's Café off Washington Street, which was located in the local pool hall downtown.

She worked as a cook at a convalescent hospital located in Lexington, which was only a couple blocks from the high school. Thelma would have me visit her during my lunch hour one or two times a week. She would have me sit down in her kitchen to eat something. She was as close as a mother to me than anyone else in my life.

Leather and Music

Grandpa's standalone garage was an interesting place with all the old things that were important to him, fifteen to thirty years ago. He saved a lot of stuff because he had space in his garage for his car, plus an extra three-foot area along the walls that were lined with big bins on either side of the garage. He must have just put things in those bins when he had no use for them anymore.

He added a work shed at the back of his garage, which was thirty feet by fifty feet. He had taken his harness shop equipment with him when he retired and moved it all into this shop. It was a great place for me to explore and learn how to do lots of handyman things.

Grandpa showed me how to make belts, and he also taught me how to take his stamping tool and use it to put designs on the leather belts. He had drawers full of buckles, rivets, and snaps with different types of belt tips. There were rolls of different kinds of cowhide along with cutting tools. I spent a lot of time out there because he had an old music box that played big, tin-metal records that had holes punched into the metal which would pluck the music bar in back of the record, as the record went slowly around. Under the music bar there was a rack which moved forward when the record's music got to the end. The rack had twelve records that played one at a time. Grandpa had a big pile of these metal records underneath the stand. Inside the music box, the records would play until a spring in the back of the machine would wind down. Then someone would have to turn the crank on the side of the big box to get the spring wound up to get the machine working again. Grandpa had this big music machine in his shop to keep the people busy and interested in the music box while he did their repairs.

Throughout the time I spent with Grandpa, I would ask him questions regarding how things worked or what he used this or that tool for. He would take the time to show me or teach me how to do things. When we would go out to the workshop, he would show me how to cut the cowhide to make different widths for belts. Then he showed me how to trim them so they wouldn't have sharp edges along the top and bottom of the belt. He taught me how to put the buckle into the end of the belt and then rivet the belt to hold the buckle in place. Then he'd show me how to use the different designing punch tools to make creative marks on the belts before they were finished.

One day when we were outside, I asked how the mower worked. Grandpa explained everything with lots of patience and that's how I learned how to take it apart and how to sharpen the blades with a metal file. He had all kinds of tools to do anything that needed fixing. He would start me on a project but I would have to finish it before I could start another project.

One day I took my back wheel brakes off my bike, and I couldn't put everything back together to make the brakes work. Grandpa told me to take the inside of the brakes apart. Then he told me to remember how the parts came out and in which order. He told me to lay out the pieces as they came out of the inside of the wheel.

Grandpa always made learning something new so fun and interesting. I was never afraid of fixing anything after that experience.

Chapter Three
Processing the Memories

After Jimmy was born, his mother, Georgia, had to go back to Lexington to live with her father, Bill Brown. She had been living with her sister and her family in Kansas City. Georgia earned money for food and paid her rent by cleaning houses in the area and helping the Elbourns.

Sister Thelma Elbourn, the oldest daughter, lived in Kansas City where she was raising three children and had a husband, Frank, with an off-and-on job as a train engineer on the Union Pacific Railroad. When Georgia asked Frank if they could keep Jimmy, he said he couldn't afford to add one more mouth to feed. The Elbourns' later moved back to Overton and bought an eighty-acre farm.

The next family who couldn't take care of Jimmy was his Uncle Dwight (who was Grandpa's oldest son). Dwight lived in Lexington with his wife, Alfreda. When Jimmy was two years old, Uncle Dwight was a seasonal farmhand and didn't make a steady income with two children (four-year-old Julie, and a second daughter, Arlene, who was my age). Dwight was trying to support his family with the help of Aunt Alfreda's income. She was a caregiver in a convalescent home. Dwight couldn't even think of trying to take Jimmy in and feed one more mouth at that time in 1942.

Grandpa's third child, Jimmy's Uncle Don, was the youngest of Grandpa's kids. In 1942, Don and his wife, Ella, were living in Iowa trying to make a living by selling Wear Ever pots and pans to local farmers. He wasn't too successful since the war had started and no one had much money due to the price of crops. On top of that, Don was getting drafted into the Army. So, there was no way Don and Ella could take care of a two-year-old boy.

Georgia was placed into a state mental hospital due to Huntington's chorea, and for the next year, Jimmy lived with Bill Brown, his grandpa. But it became too much for Bill Brown to take care of a two-year-old toddler and run his leather shop. That's when grandpa had to place three-year-old Jimmy into the orphanage.

Grandpa Adopts My Dog, Nickie

After I went to live in the orphanage, Grandpa agreed to take care of my dog, Nickie, a little black rescue dog who looked like a terrier. Every time I came to Grandpa's for the holidays, I would get out of the car and run into the house because of the fun of meeting Nickie again. He would come running towards me and jump up on my chest. Then he'd turn and want me to catch him. Of course I was too small to catch him, so we both would fall to the floor. He would lick my face, then jump out of my arms, running as fast as he could for the front door. He'd hit the screen door with his head to pop the screen door open. Then he'd run as fast as he could around the outside of the house and end up at the back screen door. He'd hit the door with his head, which made the back door pop open. Then he would grab the bottom of my pants leg and start shaking my leg until I fell down on the ground. At that time, he would jump on me, start licking my face again, and the game would start all over.

The only time Nickie would stop was when I would stand up on the dining room chair and hold my arm above my head with a treat that Grandpa had given me. This is what I had to do before Nickie got to the back door again. He would come in full speed, then jump up and take the treat out of my hand. He had to jump at least seven feet high to get the treat. He was a powerful dog, and he could take on any dog in the neighborhood. I loved him so much.

Grandpa Was Always There for Me

I had come to Grandpa's house every holiday while living in the orphanage, so I was quite comfortable in that environment. Grandpa's house had three rooms and a bath—a kitchen, living room, and a bedroom with a double bed covered with a goose down blanket. Grandpa had added a room and a screened-in porch on the side of the house facing the garage. The room had four or five storm windows, bright enough to keep his thirty parakeets warm in the winter. He also kept his washing machine and washtubs in that room.

Grandpa had been raised on the homestead farm east of town. He got married and lived there with his wife, and that's where they raised their family, just outside of Lexington. His three children now lived close by with their families because they all wanted to be close to him, since he was alone after his wife died in 1933.

Grandpa was now seventy-eight years old and had retired from his leather and harness shop business that served the local farmers and ranchers over the past fifteen years. He was a small man who always wore a light brown felt hat with a small band around the crown of the hat. During the summer, he wore a fine-woven, light-yellow straw hat. He always wore long-sleeved shirts with an arm band to keep his right forearm tight. Did I ever know why? I guess it was out of habit, or maybe it was for keeping his shirt sleeve out of his sewing machine while he worked on heavy leather products. He did lose his right index finger just at the second joint while using his sewing machine long before I lived with him in 1962.

He wore baggy dress pants with suspenders along with long-john underwear all the time. He had round, wire-rimmed glasses that hooked behind his ears. He bathed maybe twice a week and he did his own laundry without bleach once every two weeks. So his underwear wasn't too white, and his shirts weren't ironed.

He had an old washing machine with an agitator in the middle of the tub that turned back and forth. The washing machine was electric with a drain hose that dumped the dirty water out into a big metal tub. On top of the washing machine was a ringer with a double roller to wring out the clothes as you pulled them out of the water with a stick because the water was so hot. Taking the washtub of wet clothing out to the backyard, he would hang all the clothes on the line at the back of his house for the day.

He loved his front yard that was full of flowers, and each side of the sidewalk bloomed with all kinds of colored roses that adorned the path to the front door of his house. We had a lot of people stop to admire his yard. He even had his picture in the paper one year along with his multi-stem, extra-large Easter lilies. When I was maybe fourteen years old, I would help Grandpa by mowing the lawn. Before then, I wasn't big enough to push the mower because the grass was too thick.

Chapter Four
Seventh Grade Adventures

Grandpa's son, Dwight, his wife, Alfreda, and their three children: Arlene, Julie, and Ron lived only a few blocks from our house near 8th Street in Lexington. When Grandpa was not home two or three evenings a week, they would invite me over for dinner. I was happy to be around family because I didn't like being alone so much. Besides, I wasn't the greatest cook at thirteen years old, and I liked eating a home-cooked meal.

Julie was the oldest of the children, and her sister, Arlene, was two years younger. Arlene was the same age as I was—thirteen—and we were in the same grade at school. The older sister, Julie, acted as if she was the mother of Arlene as well as Ron. Their mother, Alfreda, had always worked to help support the family, and she usually showed up after work around 5 o'clock. Julie or Arlene were the ones who started the supper preparations.

We had all agreed that we would walk to school together on the first day. As we walked, Julie said, "You guys, when you get to the schoolhouse, go to the second floor and start looking for the bulletin board, which is halfway down the hallway. Find the list of classes and look for your name. Alongside your name you will see your homeroom number. That's where you need to go. Good luck and don't panic. Lots of kids will be looking for that bulletin board, and the hallway will be packed with students who are as confused as you are. It's okay. You'll do fine. Bye!"

Julie went in another direction, which meant Arlene and I had to fend for ourselves and find that bulletin board with our names on it. We climbed the stairs to the second floor, and I hung onto Arlene's hand as best I could, but with so many students pushing against us and bumping into us, I somehow lost Arlene in the crowd. As I pushed and twisted my way through the hallway of loud students, I finally arrived at the bulletin board. I stared at the list, but I didn't know anyone's name. Eventually, I found my name, which was handwritten at the bottom of the list, probably because I was new to the school system. My room number was 520, which was also handwritten next to my name.

My next challenge was to find my homeroom. First, I found room 630 so I continued walking. But the next room number was 640. I knew I was going the wrong way so I turned around and finally saw room 570. Two more doors down, I saw 520. When I walked into the room, every desk was taken. As I scanned the back of the room, I saw a couple guys leaning against the wall, so I joined them.

Standing there and not knowing anyone, one of the boys motioned for me to stand next to him. So I sauntered over, looking down at my shoes and feeling a little bit anxious.

The boy said in a quiet voice, "You must be new here. I don't remember seeing you before. My name is Monty Schrack, and I live not too far from the school. Where do you live?"

Before I could answer, the room all of a sudden became quiet when a young, small-statured lady opened the door. She walked into the room with a look of confidence. And without looking at any of us, she picked up a piece of chalk from the chalkboard tray and wrote her name on the board. Ms. Sayer. Then she introduced herself as a first-year teacher who had graduated from the University of Nebraska with a math major. She stated a lot of other accomplishments she had acquired while at the university.

Giving a quick glance at everyone around the room, she said, "You are to report to my room every morning at 8 o'clock. We will read all the announcements and then take roll call. I will establish rules for you to follow while you are in my class."

Ms. Sayer began calling names and told us if our name didn't get called, we would have to report to the main office. She called about twenty-five students who responded to their name. My name was not called. She asked for the students who didn't get called to raise their hand. There were five of us.

She told us, "Go out in the hall and wait until I come out of the classroom."

The five of us filed out into the hallway. We waited for less than ten minutes when Ms. Sayers came out of the classroom.

She told us, "Go to the office and talk to Mrs. Smith. She will get you assigned to a homeroom."

We walked to the main office where Mrs. Smith was waiting for us. She said, "I want all of you to line up single file, and then give me your name." She continued, "When you come to school tomorrow, go to the same bulletin board you used this morning. Find your name and your homeroom number. Now, go back to the room where you came from for the rest of the day."

The five of us walked into Ms. Sayer's room and one student told her what Mrs. Smith had told us. Ms. Sayer pointed to the empty chairs at the back of the room and told us to take our seats. Without even missing a beat, Ms. Sayer continued with her rules of operating a classroom. Before we were dismissed, she told us what to expect on a daily basis regarding our conduct, and then she explained her guidelines for what to expect with tests and grades.

At supper that evening, I told Grandpa all about my day, and how glad I was that it was over.

"You're a brave boy, Jimmy," Grandpa said. "Our community will surround you and make you feel welcome. You'll see."

The Second Day at My New School

The next morning, Arlene went to her homeroom and I went to the second floor. On the bulletin board, I found my homeroom number, which was the same room as yesterday. Ms. Sayers, the math teacher, was my homeroom teacher.

There were a couple empty chairs at the back of the room and I sat down just as Ms. Sayers entered. She looked around and announced, "We have a new boy in our class. His name is Jim Brown."

Everyone turned around and stared at me. It felt weird and embarrassing.

Then without missing a beat, Ms. Sayers pointed to the three piles of red books stacked on the top of her desk.

"I'll be handing out algebra books today after I take roll call," she said.

Being raised in the orphanage, I was used to having my lifelong friends around me, so it felt really strange not to know anyone. It also felt awkward not knowing the rules and procedures, but I figured someone would correct me if I wasn't doing the right thing.

Monty, whom I had met yesterday was sitting at the desk in front of me. He was about my height and had blond hair with a flattop haircut.

He turned around and asked, "Do you have an extra pencil? I forgot mine."

Fortunately, my cousin, Julie, had told me to carry two pencils and a notebook so I could write down all the instructions from my teachers. I reached into my shirt pocket and handed him one of the pencils.

At the end of class, Monty handed me my pencil and said, "I saw you walking to school today with two girls. I road my bike to school today and passed you on the way in. I live near you. After school, why don't you meet me at the bike rack and I'll walk home with you."

"OK," I said.

"What is your next class?" Monty asked. "Mine is history."

"I don't remember what my next class is or what the room number is."

Monty pointed to the spiral notebook I was holding, and said, "Look at the schedule in the back of your notebook."

I pulled out the folded schedule sheet and discovered that I had English class next.

Before I could even ask where that classroom was, Monty hollered as he headed down the hall, "English is downstairs on the right. I'll meet you after school. My last class is PE. It's over at 3:30."

***

At 3:30, I walked to the bike rack where Monty was waiting for me.

He asked, "Ready to go home?"

Monty and I talked all the way to my house. He'd ask questions, and I'd answer. Then I'd ask questions, and he'd answer. As we stood on the sidewalk in front of my house, Monty told me he lived on the same street, just one block further.

"Why don't you come home with me? I have to feed my two cats, but you can meet my mom and then I can show you my room."

"Sure, that sounds fine to me."

When we got to his house, his mom was at home, and she asked who I was. Then she said, "It's great to have you here to play with Monty."

Then Monty took me to his bedroom and opened up the bottom drawer of his dresser. I was amazed, in a good way. The drawer was filled with comic books. So, for the next forty-five minutes, we looked through different comic books. We talked about who the best hero was in the cowboy comic book: Lach Larou with his whip and Straight Arrow with his horse, Fury. We both also liked Dick Tracy and Superman.

Monty's mother suddenly opened his bedroom door and announced, "Jimmy, it's about time for you to go home to have dinner with your grandpa."

Monty said, "Jim, take a Superman comic book home with you. I can get it from you in homeroom tomorrow."

Monty walked me to the back door and said, I'll see you tomorrow in homeroom."

***

After homeroom the next morning, Monty said, "I want to introduce you to some of my neighborhood guy friends."

Most of the boys who sat at the back of the room were Monty's friends. As we approached, the bell rang for school to start and we headed to homeroom. The tallest boy sitting to the right of me was Bill Montoya. He was the same boy who had put his elbows on my desk yesterday and asked my name. Bill was Mexican with long arms covered with a long-sleeve flannel shirt. His legs were long too and they filled up the space under his desk. His hair was jet black and he needed a haircut because it covered his ears.

Bill turned his face toward me, saying, "I saw you yesterday."

The boy sitting on the other side of Bill was Larry Greenlee who was my height with wide shoulders. He had red hair with a big wave built up with "Brylcreem." He had dark green eyes and a small mouth.

He looked in my direction and said, "Hi."

The third boy Monty introduced me to was Don Hickman. He sat at the desk next to Larry. Don was very smooth in his gestures and he wore an ironed, long-sleeved white shirt with a turned-up collar at the back of his neck. His hair was trimmed with hardly a wave in the front. A small section of hair hung down on his forehead above his left eye. His dark brown eyes accentuated his long nose. He leaned forward across his desk, raised his left hand and waved at me.

"Glad to meet you. Maybe we'll see you tonight."

Yesterday, Monty had told me that all his friends went to West Ward and lived in the same neighborhood.

Then Bill Montoya said, "We'll come by on our bikes tonight to pick you up. We're going for a ride downtown."

Becoming One of the Gang

That evening after I had finished eating supper with Grandpa, there was a knock on the front screen door. I jumped up and when I got to the door, I saw Monty and Bill with two other boys, each with their own bike.

I turned to Grandpa and told him, "I'm going with my friend, Monty Schrack and several other boys to ride around a little bit. I'll be home before it gets too dark."

Grandpa said, "Be careful and stay out of trouble."

I opened the front screen door and hollered at the guys, "I have to get my bike from the backyard. I'll meet you at the end of the driveway."

As I rode my bike to the end of the driveway, the group, led by Bill Montoya, had already started out and I was at the rear following the pack of guys. The five of us rode down to Main Street. We stopped at the Texaco gas station because some of us needed air in our tires. Texaco had a red air hose laying outside where anyone could get the air for free.

Bill Montoya said, "Let's go down to the Blue Lounge and see if I can get some money from my uncle. So again, Bill led us down Main Street, but we were riding on the sidewalks because most of the people were home and not on the street. Eight blocks later, we got to the Blue Lounge, which was a beer bar. We had to wait for someone to come out the back door where we were waiting. Five or so minutes later, a man came to the back screen door. Bill approached the man and asked if he would go back in to get Bill's uncle to come to the back door. The man went back into the bar. Ten or fifteen minutes went by before his uncle showed up at the back door.

Bill asked him for some money to buy a hamburger and a coke. His uncle gave him three bucks, then turned before going back into the bar.

His uncle said, "Billy, go get something to eat, and then get yourself home without any trouble."

"Thanks," Bill said, "I will."

Bill walked up to us, and said, "Let's go and see Merle Cranfield. Hopefully he is at the café working."

We got on our bikes and followed Bill up Main Street to a building which was all lit up. There was a big white square sign with red letters, MEL'S DINER. The four of us parked our bikes and then walked up to the front door. Monty opened the door to the restaurant. Upon entering there were six tables with chairs around each table at the front of the room. Near the middle of the café was a counter that had eight chrome stools that were covered with red vinyl. Sitting at the last stool was a man who was having dinner. The boy behind the counter had broad shoulders and wore an apron with the ties in front of his stomach. He had a nice face with brown hair that was covered up with a white paper hat that sat cockeyed on his head. He was taller than me and had more meat on his bones, which made him look solid.

Merle looked up from his conversation with a customer and said, "Bill, you and the gang set over there at the first table. I'll be with you soon."

Merle then turned to his customer and asked him if he would like to have a refill on his coffee.

The man stood up, took out his billfold, laid some money on the counter, and said, "Thank you, Merle, but I have to get on my way. Keep the change. Get some good grades while you're in school this year, and say hello to your dad for me."

Merle's dad was the owner of the café. Merle worked there to help run the establishment.

Bill then turned to Merle and said, "I'd like to buy three Cokes and one Nestlé orange."

Merle got up and walked behind the counter. Rather quickly he was serving our beverages at the booth where we were sitting.

Bill asked Merle, "What time do you get off work? We want you to ride with us."

Merle said, "Between 8:30 and 9:00, when my dad gets back from running errands. By the way, who is this guy you brought along tonight? I don't know him."

Bill said, "This is Jim Brown and he lives close to Monty Schrack's house."

Merle then turned to me and asked, "Weren't you in our homeroom two days ago?"

I shook my head yes just as the phone rang. Merle went to the back of the café to answer the phone.

Bill stood up and said, "It'll be too late for us to wait for Merle before he gets off work. So, drink up, and we'll look for something else to do."

We finished our drinks, and Bill waited for Merle to get off the phone. He told him we couldn't wait around, but we'd see him another day.

Outside, we mounted our bikes and followed Bill to a street that was very dark but close to downtown.

He gathered us together and said, "We're going to do the rope trick tonight. That's why we're on a dark street. Now one of us will stand on the other side of the street, and I'll stand on this side of the street. I want you to stand in this position like you are holding a rope and pulling on it. I'll be standing over here with the same pose. When a car comes our way and sees us in his headlights, he'll think we're holding a rope from one side of the street to the other. We will get them to slam on their brakes as the car comes to a screeching halt. As soon as they slam on their brakes, run like hell and hide behind the houses."

Bill and Monty were the first to show the rest of us how it worked, for they had done this before. Two minutes later, a car came up the street with its low beam headlights shining on Billy and Monty. They looked like they had a wire or thin rope and were pulling at both sides of it. The person driving the car slammed on his brakes and we all ran to hide behind the houses. We waited until the car slowly drove off, and then we met back out on the street. We all had a good laugh seeing the trick worked.

"Let's try it again, but now it's my turn," Larry Greenlee said. "Jim, take the other side of the street."

So Larry and I set up the next fake road trick—holding the pretend rope. This time the driver slammed on his brakes, jumped out of the car, and started chasing Larry while we all ran and hid again.

The driver left his car running so he had to turn around to get back to his car. He was cussing loudly as he got in his car and drove off.

We all had a good laugh over that one, but I was glad he hadn't caught any of us.

It was getting late so I told the boys I had to go home. We split up and Monty and I headed toward our houses.

What a fun evening that was!

Later that night after I visited with Grandpa and told him about my day, I went to get cleaned up before going to bed. I had to chuckle to myself after realizing I was actually fitting into this little community and life here wasn't so bad.

I remembered my first couple days at school and having this fear of not knowing anyone. I wondered if the other students would accept me, make fun of me, or ignore me. I had no self-esteem and I avoided looking into other students' eyes even when they spoke to me. I was never taught to look at the person who was talking to me, even if it was an adult giving me instructions. In fact, I was never taught how to introduce myself to someone when I first met them. Shaking hands always felt awkward, so I didn't do it. I looked at the floor instead. But now, having a small circle of guy friends, I felt like they had kind of accepted me. Yet, I often wondered how the guys and girls from the orphanage were doing...and if they were happy.

Chapter Five
New Life Challenges

It had been a long three months since I had first entered the hallways of my new school in Lexington. Fitting in and gaining respect from fellow classmates is always a challenge, but as an orphan boy, it sometimes feels like it's a lot harder. I thought one of the easiest ways to make friends might be through participating in a sport.

The Challenge of Getting Chosen for a Tag Football Team

At school, I noticed a group of boys playing a game of tag football during our lunch recess break. They looked like they were having fun playing on the dirt playground. It was located on the south side of the school where there was only a small amount of grass growing. In reality, it was weeds, not grass.

One day I decided to stand in a lineup for the game of tag. The captain of each team would go through the line and choose the guys they wanted to play on their team. Bill spoke up and told the captain he wanted to choose me, even though I was one of the smallest boys in the lineup.

I was happy and excited to be chosen. After that day, someone would always pick me to be on a team where Bill played as an end. And sometimes I'd play on the opposite team because Bill had been chosen first because of his speed. Of course, on most days, I was second to the last guy chosen by the two team captains. Short guys like me were chosen last because of our size. Not our speed. Being chosen last was not good for my ego. So I began to wonder if I could be chosen sooner.

During some of the games, a pass was thrown in my direction, but it was intended to be received by a tall kid. The tall kids would run the ball in a straight down-and-out pattern. Instead of tagging the kid, I wanted to show the captains that I was tough. So, I'd try to tackle the runner. Or I'd purposely get into his feet as he ran to catch the ball.

On this particular day as I tackled the runner, the sliding motion caused me to hit the dirt and sharp gravel at record speed. I scraped both my elbows and feet and it hurt like heck, but I couldn't show the pain I was feeling. I usually wore long-sleeved flannel shirts that kept me from ripping open my elbows or arms. This was usually known as turf burn. To me, with all the pain I was feeling, I didn't think of it as a turf burn. I just knew I had a wound where my blood was mixed with dirt and small rocks.

I pulled out the front part of my shirt that I would normally tuck into my pants. I used the shirttail to wipe off the dark blood, dirt, and small rocks. Using the doubled-up shirt along with pushing hard on my arm above the wound helped me stop the bleeding as I got ready for the next play of tag football.

I learned fast that I had to prove myself with the other boys, so I wouldn't be chosen last. Whenever anyone who had the ball came running in my direction, I would try to tackle them around their ankles instead of trying to tackle them in their upper body. I would either purposely trip them, or I'd throw my legs into their legs as they came in my direction.

Some days when I'd ride my bike home, one of my front pockets on my shirt was torn off or there was a space where the entire pocket had been ripped off the fabric. Sometimes I even went home with no shirt sleeves, because one of the players on the opposite team had ripped my sleeve off while I was being dragged on the ground by a ball carrier. A couple of times, rough play had resulted in one of the lenses in my glasses getting lost or shattered, or the bow on my glasses had been broken. That meant grandpa would have to take me down to the Lion's Club to get new glasses.

The good part of all this was I had made new friends and I was getting chosen to play tag football with the guys. That made it all worth it.

Public School Is Not Like an Orphanage School

When you're a child who lives in an orphanage from the age of three to twelve years old, and you attend school at that orphanage, you quickly realize once you've moved out that public school is a lot different. Teachers don't seem to be as compassionate as they were in the orphanage. Yes, we learned discipline and good study habits, but the staff didn't seem as strict as they were in public school.

My first experience in a public school was in junior high when I was put into English-C class. My teacher was one of the strictest educators I had ever experienced. Her name was Mrs. Jones. Even though as students we were taught to respect our elders, Mrs. Jones asked us to call her "Grandma Jones." I thought that was a little odd, because she was definitely not like any grandma I had been around. She was tough on discipline, especially if you talked in class or didn't have the right answer to her questions.

If you missed a word on the Friday spelling test, she would make you write the word one hundred times in your notebook, and she demanded that your assignment be put on her desk by the following Monday. She had all of us in her class scared of her because if she caught you talking or doing something you weren't supposed to be doing, she would grab you by the ear and pull you to the front of the class. Then she'd give you a piece of chalk and you'd be writing on the chalkboard during the rest of the class period. Sometimes she would sling the chalk eraser at you to surprise you if you whispered in her class.

I was so scared that I did everything she required of me. The next year she transferred me to English-B, because in her eyes, I had greatly improved. Yes, she was the one who recommended the transfer. Fortunately, I got put in a class with Mylan Phelps who became my partner in a lot of classes throughout my junior high school years.

Mylan and I got into geography class with Pinkie Miller as the teacher. This teacher wouldn't look up after he started the class. We would get up out of our seats and exchange seats with each other. We would throw spitballs up on the blackboards when he was giving us a chalk lesson, but he would never turn around to see who did it. We had him so frustrated that he quit halfway through the school year.

The Challenges of Trying Out for High School Football

By the end of August, boys who were entering high school were thinking about signing up for football. Several of my friends were encouraging me to sign up because of my toughness. I wasn't sure if I wanted to sign up though. I knew from various conversations that the football equipment was left over after the varsity and freshman teams were fitted out. I didn't really care if the equipment was used rather than new, since I rarely had the privilege of anything new. However, for safety's sake, I was concerned about the materials that were used for the shoulder pads, the helmets, the pants, and leg pads.

Nevertheless, or maybe in spite of the age of the used equipment, I decided to sign up for the team. I knew I was one of the smallest boys on the team, but I was happy knowing I'd be with the gang that I was running with in my neighborhood. Most of all, those boys were signed up, and I wanted to be accepted. Because Mr. Lancaster, my driver's ed teacher, knew my name was the final reason why I signed up.

I weighed all of seventy-two pounds and that was with my equipment on. So of course I didn't play much, except for scrimmages. Mr. Harrington, the football coach, put me on defense. The bigger seventh and eighth graders who made the first team in practice would see if they could run over us. The scrubs, which I was one of them, would try to run the opponent plays against the first team.

At the end of the season, when Lexington Junior High was playing McCook's Junior High team, our team scored fourteen to nothing into the fourth quarter. Mr. Harrington decided the scrub team should get in the game for all their dedication during the football season. He wanted us to get some playing time in with only two minutes left in the game. The first play McCook ran, once I was on the field was a sweep around my end, for I was supposed to be the outside line backer. The

McCook's halfback was leading their fullback and went to block Bill Montoya, who was the defenses' end. Bill was twice as tall and with his speed, he blocked. Both players were knocked to the ground. That left me as the only one to stop the fullback who was coming right at me. I put my helmet down, intending to go directly for his knees and shoes. Unfortunately, I didn't know where my arms were. I tackled him and he fell forward. He rolled me over backwards, and I felt like I was going to pass out.

I was close to the sideline when I heard the voice of Logan Lancaster, our driver's ed teacher shouting, "Get up, Jimmy. Get up, Jimmy. You made a great tackle."

As I rolled over to get to my knees, I pushed hard to get to my feet. I looked over, and there was Logan Lancaster. He was one of the teachers who was helping Mr. Harrington with the team on game days. I didn't think anyone knew what my name was except the coach who called me "Brown." So I got up ready for the next play, which went around the other end. Of course, I didn't get in the tackle. I was pulled off the field after that second play.

As I ran off the field, Mr. Lancaster came over and patted me on my butt, saying, "Good job, Jimmy!"

At that moment, I felt like I was the biggest guy on the field, and I could tackle anyone. That was the highlight of my football career at Lexington High School. It was our last game of the season.

Winning at Fishing

The summer before eighth grade I was spending time with my cousins, Julie and Arlene. They had parts in the town's summer theater performance. Julie and Arlene took me over to the girls who wanted to rehearse their parts in the performance. The girls lived near the high school and were practicing their parts in the front yard of their home. To tease the girls, Steve Smith, who lived down the street, started riding his bike back and forth in front of their house while yelling playful things to interrupt their rehearsal. I think they knew he meant no harm.

After three or four times of riding past, he stopped and hollered at me, "Jimmy, get on your bike and follow me to my house."

We got to his house which was only a block away. We walked into the kitchen through the back door, and he announced, "I'm thirsty."

He opened the refrigerator and got out a big milk bottle and poured two glasses. After we had a few gulps of milk, he told me he wanted to go to my house, because I had made a comment that I had fishing gear that my grandfather had given me. So when we got on our bikes and rode to my house, I took him out to the garage. We looked in the storage bins, and we found a big fishing net rolled up with two long poles.

We talked a little and he said, "Wouldn't it be fun to go to the river and see if we could catch some fish?"

"It does sound like fun, but I'll need to ask Grandpa if I can go."

Steve said, "I have to go home. I have chores to do before my mother gets home. But I'll come over in the morning, and maybe your grandpa will let you go fishing with me."

Steve came over the next morning, and I asked Grandpa if we could go to the river on our bikes with the fishing net. Grandpa usually never said much, but today he told me to be home before dinner.

We peddled our bikes and carried the net to the river. We ran into a friend of Steve's named Mike Sladkey. He had fished this one pond that was located right alongside the Platte River Bridge. Mike told us he didn't catch any fish out of that hole. So Mike went to another fishing hole to use his fishing skills.

Steve and I didn't tell Mike about our net, but after Mike left, we went down to the same pond where Mike had fished. We unrolled the netting, and it was long enough that I could stand on one side of the pond with Steve standing on the other side of the pond. We dropped in our net and pulled the net very slowly towards the end of the pond. We caught at least thirty fish of all different sizes. We took the largest ones and put them on a stringer. The smaller ones we threw back into the pond. Then we went over to where Mike was fishing and showed him our stringer of ten big fish. We told him we got them out of the fishing hole he had just left. We told him we used fish guts as bait. Mike immediately went back to the same pond using fish guts. We packed up grandpa's net with the stringer of fish and peddled back home. Mike kept fishing that same hole the rest of the day but didn't catch anything.

Steve has been a friend who has introduced me to a lot of firsts in my life.

One week later, on a Saturday, Steve had ridden his bike over to my house to play Army. After a while, he asked me if I would come with him to his house. So, I followed him home.

Once at Steven's house, we walked inside and Steve hollered, "Is anybody home?"

His mother left notes on the door of the refrigerator with chores Steve had to do before she got home. Steve grabbed the notes and then took me upstairs into his bedroom which shared a closet with his older brother, Bruce. Steve told me he needed a clean pair of jeans, so he opened the closet. What I saw shocked me. There were at least nine or ten pairs of jeans piled up on the floor. I owned two pair of jeans, and I thought I was lucky.

Steve dug through the pile of jeans until he apparently found a pair he liked. He pulled off his dirty jeans and climbed into the pair he found on the floor. Several minutes later, Bruce came home and ran up the stairs.

He took one look at me and then glared at Steve, screaming, "Steve, what are you doing with my jeans on?"

Steve said, "These are my jeans."

"No, these are my jeans," shouted Bruce.

Within a split second, Bruce threw his arm around Steve's neck and flipped him over his hip. Steve landed on his back on top of the pile of jeans. Steve grabbed Bruce's right leg and pulled it forward bringing Bruce down landing on his butt with his back up against the wall. Then he slammed Bruce's head against the wall. They both stood up and started slugging at each other.

After Steve hit Bruce on the side of his face, Bruce said, "Okay, you can wear those jeans today, but I will wear them tomorrow."

I had never seen anything like this between brothers. In the orphanage, the brothers I knew were usually fighting alongside each other not with each other.

The minute Bruce was gone, Steve and I rode our bikes to the high school to play basketball with the other guys at Dick Shaw's basketball court.

Climbing Trees and Boy Scout Adventures

You might be wondering if the life of an orphan boy is anything like a boy who grows up in a family with two parents. I feel like I was lucky because I had my grandpa and we lived in a rural area. Not living in a big city brings lots of benefits to a young boy, one of which is being able to play outside and enjoying your friends. Remember, in the time I was growing up, we didn't have computers, cell phones, or any type of communication other than a telephone or someone ringing the dinner bell or hearing your name called from across the neighborhood.

I had many opportunities to explore all the treasures young boys love when I went rummaging around in my grandpa's garage. In fact, during the spring of seventh grade, on one Saturday morning, I found a lot of random pieces of wood and two-by-fours. I also found wood along the property line of our next door neighbor that would be perfect for my plans of making a tree house.

"Hey, Monty," I called to my friend who was helping me find wood, "which tree around here should we choose?"

I climbed onto the roof of grandpa's shed and stared into the distance looking for a big oak tree. It would need to have huge limbs. Then there it was, the perfect oak tree.

"Look, Monty," I said, pointing to the old oak tree.

"Perfect," Monty wailed. "But we're going to need to round up other guys to help us."

Before lunchtime, four of us were bringing the two-by-fours to the side of grandpa's shed. We used a ladder to get the wood to the roof, and then we carried the wood across the roof to the big tree we decided to use as the base. Then we nailed the wood to the tree where we planned to build the treehouse.

Monty and two of my other friends were wrapping wire around the boards to attach to the tree, which would secure the base of our treehouse. We brought up flat boards to put on top of the two-by-fours. As the guys were all busy doing that, I went out to grandpa's garage alongside the storage bins and found a four-man Army tent. I also found a radio with headphones that plugged into the nonoperative radio console.

We hauled the tent up to the tree branch that now had a makeshift floor, and we tied ropes to hold up the top of the tent. Then we brought up the radio and headphones along with a short table we had found in the neighborhood. We set up the inside of our treehouse and called it our headquarters. It would be the perfect spot for our game of Army on Saturdays and Sundays.

The whole neighborhood gang came over the following Saturday. They brought their guns and rifles along with any Army gear they had at home. To get inside the headquarters, you had to climb a ladder up to the roof of grandpa's shed. Then you had to walk over the top of the shed to the big limb of the tree. Next, you'd step up into headquarters. So, on the weekends, we spent a lot of time choosing sides, making rules, and going out on "Army" missions.

What Does a Tree Mean to a Boy?

Let's talk about trees and memories I'll never forget. Ever since I was a kid in the orphanage, I loved to climb trees. First, there's the challenge to get to the first branch. To begin with, it takes a few times to figure out the placement of your hands as well as the placement of your feet to climb the trunk to the first branch. I'll always remember the smell of the bark and the feel of my hands and arms as I hugged the trunk of my favorite tree.

Patience when positioning your body while you're climbing trees is important so you don't fall unexpectantly to the ground and end up getting hurt. Your arms must be strong enough to hold you and pull your body up to the next branch. It's a challenge and a goal to be achieved when you can develop the ability to get your arms and legs to work together to get from one branch to another.

The second part of climbing the tree is finding a passage up the tree after you get to the first branch. Reaching for the right branch and the action you take to hold your head and body in the best position is crucial as you climb the branches to the top.

The third most important thing to consider is where to place your feet on the branches. You don't want to wedge the sole of your shoe too tightly against the tree. So, instead of wearing tennis shoes, it's best if you wear hard sole leather shoes.

The fourth choice is where to stop climbing, because the higher you go, the thinner the branches are, which means those thin branches might not support your weight in the tree. If you get too high on the tree, or if your head is above the tree, you could get too much sunshine and you'd end up with a sunburn. When you climb up that high, you soon realize there's no place to rest your body. If you need to rest while you're climbing, you must find a fork branch that is parallel to the ground to place your butt on. That way, the two forks and your back are against the main branch of the tree for support. In this position, your feet do not have to be on one branch for support.

There are many benefits for sitting still in a tree. One is that you will feel the sway of the tree when the wind ebbs and strengthens. If you sit long in silence, you will start experiencing the birds darting and hopping branch to branch as well as their singsong talking. You will be able to listen to the wind sounds and the leaves fluttering. You will hear different sounds from other trees because of their placement of each tree to the direction of the wind flow. Some sounds are high and some sounds are low, depending upon the type of tree.

The smell of the air is a sweet scent due to the wind flowing through the fluttering leaves. The sound of children playing in the nearby playground flows in and out as the velocity of the wind varies throughout the time you're setting in the tree. You can feel the freedom of not being stuck to the ground because of gravity.

One of the most important feelings is to let your imagination go free. Up in that tree you are not confined to other people's demands or comments. You begin to know the freedom of being a bird. Birds can go wherever they want, and they can set as long as they want. A bird's main concern is finding something to eat. You can escape your enemies and show off your beautiful body to other birds. And you won't get laughed at because of your silliness. If I were a bird, I would learn how to hang upside down on a branch, and I would be the belle of the ball. This is why boys love to climb trees!

Boy Scout Adventures

During the summer after seventh grade, Merle Cranfield invited me to go to a Boy Scout meeting over at the Presbyterian church, which was right around the corner from my house. Merle Cranfield's dad, along with two other dads, Mr. Hock and Mr. Derickson, were the scout masters. At the meeting, the scout masters had planned an outing where they would take the troops. We were going on a hike to the Platte River, which was one and a half miles from town. It was decided we'd camp out Saturday night, and then we'd walk back home the next morning.

Mr. Hock approached me after the meeting and asked, "Jim, would you like to go on the outing with us?"

"Yes!" I said with a lot of excitement.

"Okay, then meet at the church Saturday morning at 10 o'clock."

I went home and told grandpa, who then took me out to the garage. He began digging around in the side bins of the garage, which I already knew was where he kept almost everything he ever owned.

He said, "Jimmy, you'll be sleeping outdoors, and you'll need a tarp and a blanket. Go in the house and look in the hall closet above the hanging clothes. You'll find a wool blanket that is red, black, and yellow. Grab it and bring it to me."

So I ran as fast as I could into the house. I found the blanket and bolted out the door, heading to the side of the garage where Grandpa was waiting.

Grandpa nodded at me as if giving me his approval that I had found the blanket.

"I have a tarp here in the bin that you can use to place down on the ground when you get to the campsite. Then all you have to do is put your blanket on top of it."

We found the tarp after moving some things around. I spread out the tarp and placed the blanket on top of it. Then grandpa showed me how to tuck the sides of the tarp over the edges of the blanket. He rolled them up into a small roll, then tied twine string around the roll at each end. In one of his bins in the garage, he found a small black iron skillet along with a camping spoon attached to the fork.

Grandpa said, "It's a spoon and fork. You keep it in your inside chest pocket, and we will hang the skillet from the hook that I am making for your Army belt."

***

I met with the troop that Saturday morning. All the boys were wearing their Boy Scout shirts tucked into their jeans. I was the only one who had a red flannel shirt not tucked into my blue jeans. I had a bedroll over my shoulder with the skillet hanging from my belt. As we walked the one and a half miles to the river, I would be the first to admit that I knew nothing about camping or walking in formation.

When we got to the campsite, we dug a pit that would be used as our outdoor fireplace to keep us warm. We gathered branches and twigs and tossed them into the pit. We didn't have tents, so we arranged our blankets around the fire pit. The scout master showed us how to make scrambled eggs along with bacon and toast on a stick. After our meal, we explored the banks of the river and saw a beaver's den made out of tree limbs chopped up and arranged by the beavers. We hiked some more and found various types of animal tracks along the river banks.

I barely slept that night because I kept hearing all the animal noises throughout the night. The air was cold and it was cold outside the next morning.

The next day was Sunday and we packed everything up and walked back home. I visited with Grandpa a little bit and thanked him for all the help he had given me so I could go on my first Boy Scout overnight adventure.

I was so tired when I got home late that afternoon that I went to bed after talking to Grandpa. I slept through the whole night.

On Monday morning, I looked back on my Boy Scout event and I was happy to have met a lot of new people. I did learn a lot about camping too, and I loved being out in nature, but that was nothing new for me. I've always liked being outside.

I attended every meeting of the troop after the campout. Aunt Thelma bought me a Boy Scout shirt and sewed on the patches that needed to be on the shirt. At the end of the summer, the troop went to Camp Augustine (a Boy Scout camp) in Grand Island for a whole week of activities.

The first night, we slept in an eight-man tent, which means there were eight cots in each tent in the Lexington campsite troop, which consisted of two tents. In my tent was Gary Neff, Bill Montoya, Rod Hock, Bob Ernst, Jim Ernst, Stanley Derickson, and myself. Boys being boys, there was always a farting contest going on in each tent. Two categories: first, who made the most noise, and second, who made the biggest stink.

At dawn, as the sun came up and shined on the east side of our tent, I opened my eyes and looked around. Everybody was quiet in the tent. Then all of a sudden, I heard some quick movements at the north end. When I raised up on my elbows, I saw two or three of the boys jump up.

One boy hollered, "Oh my god! Oh my god!"

Then a whole group of boys dashed toward the exit wearing only their jockey shorts. Stan Derickson was still asleep but he had let out the most raunchiest fart. You could almost see the fumes. As the gas smell traveled up to my end of the tent, boys were waking up. Some were coughing and gagging. When the smell got to Bill Montoya, he jumped up and then vomited on the ground next to his cot. Stan was the champion for the whole week.

***

Boy Scouts opened a whole new world for me, because of the people I met. The next summer, our troop went to Colorado with a goal of climbing Long's Peak, where we were camped out. It took us two days to get to the top and back down to base camp. Our troop was very active and some of the boys got to go to Valley Forge for the Boy Scout Jamboree.

Gary Neff and Rod Hock earned enough merit badges to become Eagle Scouts, which is the highest rank in all of scouting. After Boy Scouts at age fifteen, when the Boy Scouts go to a higher group for boys, they become Explorer Scouts.

Explorer Scouts had meetings within the local Lexington Volunteer Fire Department station. One of our main jobs was to lay out cable wire from specific areas during a fire or a catastrophe to maintain communications between the fire chief and the volunteer firemen. There were no cell phones during that time, and we had only landlines which got overloaded when the community was making an excessive number of calls. Our troop remained together for approximately four years.

***

You might wonder where I got my courage to try all these new things at such a young age. The way I look at it, there are a lot of opportunities given to you almost every day. You don't have to be afraid to say yes. We all have gifts given to us at birth that help us be the person we're meant to be. When you take a chance, as long as it's not risking your life, you can move forward with confidence, or say no, or stop. You'll know by your intuition what is the right and the wrong thing to do. If you hesitate, then don't do it.

What you get out of an experience is you get to know yourself better—what you like or dislike to continue on with life. You want to welcome mistakes or failures only if you learn from the experience and can make a better decision the next time around.

I would tell any young boy to join the Cub Scouts and then become a Boy Scout following into Explorers. There is a lot to learn from this organization, even if you do not have a dad. By becoming a Boy Scout, I got to see a lot of dads who cared for their boys with different methods of motivating their sons. Merit badges teach you how to gain more control of different stresses you have in your lifetime. I have modelled my family as a grown man after what I saw and experienced while in scouting.

Chapter Six

A Community Supports an Orphan

Jimmy thought back to his life at the orphanage and how he was allowed to spend most of his summers on Uncle Frank and Thelma's farm, two miles east of Overton. Their son, Terry, was three years older than Jimmy, but he was the closest Jimmy ever came to having a brother.

One time, Terry told Jimmy, "I'm going to be working for the alfalfa mill, and I'd like you to ride with me tomorrow. So, get ready to get up at 6:00 a.m."

The next morning Terry drove to pick Jimmy up, and they rode around the fields of alfalfa in his truck. They followed alongside the hay chopper that filled up his truck with cut alfalfa until his truck was full. Then we would drive to the drying mill. At the mill, Terry would dump his truckload into the hay catcher, which would raise up slowly for the load of wet alfalfa to slide into the burners. The burners were one hundred feet long and had a rotating tub where the alfalfa was constantly moving around the gas-heating unit. The alfalfa was being heated to remove the moisture from the leaves and stems of the plants.

When the dried alfalfa came out of the heating tub, the alfalfa was sucked through a big tube into the packing shed where the guys had to put this fine powder into gunny sacks. Then they sewed the top of the bag with a stitchery machine.

Sometimes Terry had to work in the bagging room. Those days he would come home covered with green powder. It was so funny for the next two or three days, because when he would blow his nose, green mucus would come out.

***

During the summer after Jimmy finished seventh grade, Terry had talked to the crew chief of the detasseling team who worked out of Overton every summer. Their job was to go through farmers' fields and pull tassels out of the tops of the cornstalks. The seed corn companies had this done every summer so they could produce seed corn for the farmers the next year.

Terry, along with the crew chief, decided that I was too short to reach the top of the stalks of corn to get to the tassel. The crew chief said he would hire me to be the water boy. My job was to fill about eight to ten canvas bags with cold well water and ride around in the semi-cattle truck. The truck was cleaned out to accommodate the working crew who brought their clothes and lunchboxes to the fields. Then the crew was driven in the truck and brought back to Overton at the end of each day. The truck driver, Wyan, would drive to a specific cornfield, and the crew chief would get the crew going through the cornfield. Each crew member was given the task of pulling the tassel out of every stalk of corn in the two rows they were assigned by the crew chief. The crew would get to the other end of the short fields, then turn around and get assigned two more rows of cornstalks. Then they would come back towards me. I would have cold water waiting for the crew when they came out of the cornfield.

Some of the cornfields were a mile long. The truck driver and I would drive around to the other end of the field. I would go to the pump house to fill all my bags to be ready with the cold ice water. By the time I would meet the crew at the other end, some of the girls would almost pass out due to the heat and the muddy soft ground they had to walk through as they picked the tassels off the tops of the cornstalks.

I did this job for eight to ten hours a day unless it rained. Then we would go home early. The time spent doing this job lasted between six to eight weeks. Making hybrid corn was a very precise process and it had to be done right. The pay was good and it allowed me to make enough money to buy all the clothes I needed for school the next fall.

Learning to Shine Shoes

As summer slipped by and August indicated it was time for school to start, I was in eighth grade. I was assigned to the B group, which was a completely different group from the C group that I had been assigned to when I reported to school my first year. I now knew a lot of the boys and I got to chum with them during the summer.

At the end of summer, after getting to know Merle Cranfield in scouting as well as during neighborhood gang meetings, he asked me if I would like to shine shoes with him at Niemi Shoe Repair Shop. Merle and I rode our bikes downtown to First Street, also called Main Street. It was located off Highway 30. Niemi's Shoe Repair Shop is on the corner, and the building is all white brick with dark green wood all around the windows and doors.

As you walked up the three steps to the front door, you were greeted with a large gold lettered sign on the door. It said Niemi Shoe Repair Shop. As you stepped inside, the floor was covered with light brown linoleum, and on your right was a shoeshine stand made of dark wood. It had six straight-back, wooden chairs on the top step. On the first step were twelve metal shoe stands. The first and second steps were covered with dark green linoleum as you climbed up to sit in the chairs.

Underneath each chair was a set of two, long shoe brushes made out of black horsehair. Underneath the shoe stands were six drawers with chrome handles. That's where the shoe polish and shoeshine rags were placed after each shoeshine had been given. The room was filled with a smell of black shoe dye, along with a burnt leather aroma from the shoe repair shop—grinding and cutting leather soles and then stitching the soles to the leather tops of the shoes. A display case and counter separated the customers from the three green dangerous machines that were located along the length of the back wall.

Mr. Niemi and his son, Charlie, were of the same stature with dark black hair. They wore heavy brown leather aprons that hung by a string from their neck and were tied in front of them. Each man had little bulges of their stomach pooching out due to the string tie that was wrapped around their bodies. Mr. Niemi, who was the father, wore gold wire rim glasses, had dark skin, deep facial lines around his aged face, and he sported a small, light grayish mustache. His hands were as black as his hair due to all the shoe dye he used to trim the soles of the shoes after they'd been stitched to the shoe tops. Most of the farmers in our area had new rubber heels and soles put on their shoes.

Mr. Niemi spoke with a broken accent from his native country, Italy. Charlie was Mr. Niemi's youngest son. He looked like his dad, but he had a nicer personality that everyone seemed to like. They both wore dark green shirts with matching pants as a uniform. Repaired shoes were cheaper than buying a new pair of shoes.

It took me two Saturdays to learn the rules of the shop and my free labor allowed me to learn how to shine shoes. All shoes brought in for repair had to be scrubbed with shoe soap, dried, and placed upon a shoe stretcher. There were about six stretchers that were screwed into the wall about chest high, next to the small shoeshine area. On Saturday mornings, we would get busy and start scrubbing and shining, mostly farmers' shoes. Then we'd lace up work shoes which was not any fun. The shoe did not take a shine.

As the walk-in customers would come through the door, a little bell tinkled over the door molding letting us know that someone was coming in the door. Most customers for shoeshines would climb up into their favorite chair, and we would come out wearing our cotton aprons, which hung around our neck and were tied in the middle of our stomachs with string. The aprons were long enough to cover our knees.

There was a method to shining shoes and a lot of extra movements were required to get that extra dime for a tip. A shoeshine cost fifteen cents, and hopefully the customer would flip you a quarter and say, "Keep the change, sonny." It took me a month or two along with Merle giving me tips on how to work the brushes, popping the shine rag, and spitting on the top of the shoe as the rag was popped two to three times over the top of the toe as well as the back of the shoe. To wind up the show, we put a black liquid on a toothbrush and went around the sole of the shoe to make it shine a darker black than the rest of the shoe.

In those days, a silver half dollar was what we were looking for from all our high tippers. Yes, all our conversations were directed towards the customer's busy day or his coming weekend activities. We never talked about ourselves, unless asked by the customer. I worked every Saturday at the Niemi Shoe Repair Shop for two-and-one-half years. Our work hours were from eight in the morning till nine that night. Our salary was six dollars for the day, plus tips. We were lucky to go home with twelve to fifteen dollars on a good day. On rainy Saturdays, we made less money.

The way I looked at this job was that I learned new skillsets at Niemi Shoe Repair. Not only did I learn how to properly shine shoes, but I learned how to amp-up my customer service skills. I always had fun while I was working. By developing the gift of talking to my customers, I got to know their attitude and thoughts about many subjects they liked to talk about. I challenged myself to remember their names, so the next time they came in, I could greet them by their name. I also learned a very important business rule: don't discuss religion, politics, or sex. Your conversation will always end up in a negative outcome for you or your customer.

I learned how to make people smile before they got off the shine stand and when they were getting ready to pay.

Number one, popping your shine rag two to three times with snapping sounds works wonders at impressing customers. Number two is always get your brushes to click with the two-one rhythm when you are buffing the shoes front and back followed by the shine rag.

Chapter Seven
It's All about Relationships in Eighth Grade

When school is out for the day, many of the kids who have a quarter in their pocket walk six blocks downtown to Stuart's Drug Store. There was a soda fountain with ten stools in front of the counter, and further into the store were five booths along one outside wall. A few of the kids would hang out at Stuart's until 4:30 or 5:00 p.m. until everyone had to go home for supper. We would get to the drug store and scramble to get a booth. All the girls would sit in their booths, which usually only left one available booth for the boys.

These were mostly seventh and eighth graders along with a few older girls because the athletic boys were practicing football or other sports at school. None of the kids in town had cars, so we all walked downtown after school. The things we ordered from the soda fountain were wild—mainly fizzes, sodas, and floats. Sometimes two or three girls would pool their money together and order a banana split for fifty cents. Fizzes and sodas were ten cents. Green River fizzes, lime soda, and a root beer float was fifteen cents. We must have driven the people who worked behind the soda fountain crazy with the different combinations of flavors we would order.

***

Girls were now included in my social activities...not that I dated them, but they were just there and I was certainly aware of them. I think that's about the time when I developed my sex hormones. And what I can share with you is while I was living at the orphanage, no one taught us kids about sex or the facts of life. For sure, Aunt Thelma and Grandpa weren't bringing up the subject either.

The first girl I became aware of in my life in Lexington was Sally Lancaster. She was Dave Gilbert's girlfriend. Dave was one of the guys I played basketball with at Monte Kiffin's house. Sally was a cheerleader for the freshman football team. Every afternoon, Sally and a group of girls would walk together to Stuart's. My friends Monte and Larry Greenlee and I would walk behind the girls. Sally was always asking questions, trying to get to know everyone.

One afternoon Sally came up to me and said she knew someone who wanted to get to know me. I didn't even think anyone knew who I was, except the boys that I ran with during after-school hours. Sally asked me for my phone number, which I wrote down on a scrap of paper. I gave her my number without any thought of what she had said or asked of me.

One early Saturday morning two weeks later, the phone rang. I answered it and the caller wanted to know if I liked banana splits. This female voice on the other end of the line was someone who asked if I knew who she was. I couldn't even guess. She said she sees me every day at the drug store after school. She was giving me clues, but I still couldn't guess who she was.

This girl was so nice, and she kept asking a lot of questions about me. One of the questions was what I was doing the rest of the morning. Finally she told me her name was Judy Edward. We ended the conversation with "maybe we can get together at the drug store next week." We did see each other at the drug store, but I had to set on the other side of the booth with Dick Shaw and Dave Gilbert so the other girls across the table wouldn't get teased by the girls in the other booths.

Sally, Judy, and Carol started talking about our class dance coming up in a couple of weeks. These quiet girls were looking at us strangely, but how did we know we were canon fodder to fill in the gaps until the real football players (hopefully) got around to asking these girls to the dance? I knew I could dance like a cool dude, where most of the jock-type football players couldn't move their feet or hips at all. The reason I could dance so well was because my cousins, Arlene and Julie, would practice with me. We would experiment with fast dances and we learned how to dance with a partner for a slow dance.

Judy never did get a date with me, but I did get together with Sally at Judy's house one Saturday afternoon.

Judy was practicing her lessons when she stopped and asked, "Which songs do you like?"

I said, "I really don't have a favorite but would you play one of your favorites?"

She turned to the piano and then started playing "Autumn Leaves."

To this day, I love that piece of music, which reminds me of her at her piano.

I spent a lot of afternoons after school walking with Sally and Judy to the drug store. The three of us would talk about events and who was who in our classes. I was so naive I never thought about asking a girl on a date. I would talk to Judy on the phone, but after a while, she wouldn't answer the phone when I'd call. I took that as a sign, and I stopped talking to Sally and Judy.

Finding Your Forever Friend

Dick Stuckey. His body structure was thin and it looked like his arms and legs were made out of steel springs. His face was long and thin, and he had a short nose and tiny ears. He always wore his hair short, with the front end combed up into a small mound of hair. Another outstanding feature was his deep resonating voice. It sounded like he spoke the truth with every word he said. He sounded knowledgeable and informative.

I met him at a Boy Scout meeting that was held at the Presbyterian church located across the alley, on the corner lot in the back of grandpa's house. At one of the Boy Scout meetings, which were held on Monday evening after school, Dick asked me if I would like to go to church with him on Sunday. I had nothing else to do on Sunday morning, so I said yes. The next Sunday, I had forgotten about it, but there was a bang on the front door around 9:00 a.m. I had just gotten up and was having breakfast with Grandpa. Breakfast consisted of Cream of Wheat with bread, thick with butter, cinnamon, and sugar sprinkled on top of the bread. Then I would put the bread in the oven and let it melt until the entire slice of bread was toasted. I'd also have a glass of milk.

I rose from the table to go open the front door, and there to my surprise was Dick Stuckey, who was wearing a white shirt and a pair of brown slacks.

When I opened the door, he said, "Are you ready to go to church with me?"

I didn't give it a second thought, but I had a blue striped flannel shirt on, with blue jeans rolled up three times at the bottom of each leg of the pants.

Dick said, "Go in and tell Grandpa you're going to church with me."

I poked my head into the house and told Grandpa I was going to church with Dick. We walked through Grandpa's yard to the back of the lot because the church was across the back alley.

As we walked through the front yard, Dick said, "You sure have a lot of flowers in your yard. Does your grandpa take care of all these flowers?"

I shrugged my shoulders, mumbling, "Yes, it's one of his hobbies, but I have to mow the yard with the push mower."

Dick said, "What is a push mower?"

As we walked around the garage. I pointed to the mower, which was propped up against the side of the garage. We continued on across the empty lot heading toward the church lot. The church building was two stories high and it cast a big, long shadow into the field we were walking through. Our shoes got wet from the dew that was still in the long grass of the fall season. Dick seemed to know where he was going because he just opened the back door of the church and we walked into the church hall.

The first room on the left was an open room with chairs stacked along the side of the room.

Dick said, "Follow me, Jimmy. We have to go to Sunday school first."

We walked up the stairs to the second floor and entered the second room on the right. He went in first and I tagged behind.

He turned to me and whispered, "Be quiet. We're late, and we need to sit at the back of the room."

I followed him and found two folding chairs that were empty at the back of the room. We sat and listened to the lady telling a Bible story about Moses crossing the river with his people. I knew this story by heart for we had heard this story at the orphanage church every year and there were always questions and answers. At the end of the class, Dick seemed to know everybody in the room and said hi to a couple of kids as we left to go down the stairs to the church entrance.

As we got to the church entrance, a man approached Dick and said, "Good morning to you. Your mother and father have already arrived."

I was one step behind Dick as I followed him into the church. We went to the center aisle of the church, and I slid into the back pew.

Dick then turned to me and said, "I'll be right back. I have to say hello to my parents to let them know I'm sitting in the back."

He then walked to the front of the church to the second pew from the front. There was a man and a woman sitting at the end of the pew. Dick bent over and said a few words to the couple. Then Dick walked back to where I was sitting and sat down beside me. After the church sermon, Dick and I were the first to be ushered out the door.

As we were leaving, Dick said, "Jimmy, I'm going to meet my parents now and then go home with them. So I'll see you next Sunday."

I said, "I'll see you. Thanks."

I went around the big brick building into the alley, turned left, and went back home to have lunch with Grandpa. I talked with him and asked him why he thought someone would go out of their way to include another person in something they were passionate about. He reminded me that everyone has a guardian angel and each of us has a purpose.

"Listen to your heart, Jimmy. That's why you were created—to be good to yourself and to love others."

Embraced by Members of the Community

Every afternoon at school, I would always go over to the bike rack in front of the school building. I wanted to make sure my bike was in the rack, because it was the only thing I ever owned that meant something to me.

One afternoon after a tough tackle with Dick Carr at football practice, who had legs longer than I was tall, I broke the dark brown bow of my glasses. He had run straight through me, rolling me up into a ball like dust, and then I rolled on the ground. The right bow broke and the short end of the hinge on my glasses went into the side of my head just outside of my eye. It caused a small cut, which was bleeding down the side of my face.

Mylan Phelps helped pick me up. He dusted me off, and said, "Kid, you better go sit by the bike rack and rest."

As I was wiping the dirt and blood off the side of my face with my shirttail, Dick Stuckey came over and asked me how I was doing.

He said, "Hey, you're tough! You know how to hold your own. How is your shoulder? You really cut Carr at the kneecaps with that shoulder of yours."

Just then the school bell rang and Dick said, "Come on, let's go to class. I'll come by Sunday and we can go to church again. Is that all right?"

I said yes.

The next Sunday after church, Dick asked, "Could you ask your grandpa if you could go home with me and have lunch at my house?"

Before I could answer, he was walking alongside me.

Dick said, "Let's you and I walk over to grandpa's and ask him."

So we walked to the alley and crossed the open grass that we always walked on Sunday morning. He followed me into the house through the front door, which opened up into the little living room and dining area. Grandpa was sitting at the table, playing solitaire.

He looked up from his cards and said, "What you boys up to?"

I said, "Grandpa, Dick wants me to go have lunch with him at his house. Is it okay?"

Grandpa looked at Dick, scanning him from head to toe and said with a big smile, "Sure. Dick, do you think you can handle Jimmy?"

Dick said, "He hasn't given me any trouble yet."

We all laughed, and then I followed Dick out the front door. As we walked to the church, I saw Dick's dad standing out in front of the church waiting for us.

His dad said, "Who is this boy with you?"

Dick said, "This is Jimmy Brown, the toughest guy in town."

Dick's dad was wearing a dark brown suit with a white shirt and small thin tie. He stood a few inches taller than Dick. Dick introduced him to me as Lyman. Then we climbed into their blue, four-door station wagon. The three of us sat in the front seat, and Dick's dad drove north on Lincoln and turned left on 17th Street. Then we drove into their driveway which led into their property. The property was surrounded by a white, three-foot-high fence. The driveway was long and led into the garage, which was a separate structure in back of the main house. After we parked, we went into the house through the back door and entered the kitchen where I met Mrs. Stuckey and Dick's little sister, Susan.

It seems to me that most of the boys who were in my class had little sisters. Paul Diefenbach (Faith), Steve Smith (Marge), Rod Hock (Debbie) and Gary Neff (Patty) had little sisters. Little sisters were someone you always had to worry about. You didn't want them to get into your dealings, but they had to be taken care of, especially when moms were going out shopping or to the neighbors.

Whenever I was invited to somebody's house, whatever we were doing, there was always a little sister in the other room or out on the porch. She would watch every move we made so she could report back to her mom if we were into things we shouldn't be into. I guess that's the dilemma of having a sister. You have to make deals with your little sister or you teased your little sister. You had to make her promise not to tell everything that was happening while the big boys played. You didn't want her talking about how she overheard your discussions about neighbors, girls, coaches, or the bad words we used in our conversations. To me, little sisters were wonderful to have because of the love they provided and the devotion they showed to their bigger, teenage brother.

Mrs. Stuckey said, "You boys run upstairs and play. Lunch will be ready in half an hour."

Dick pulled on my sleeve and motioned to me to follow him as we went around the corner to go upstairs to his bedroom. When we got to his bedroom, I was in a different world. He had two beds with bedspreads that matched the wallpaper with different sailing ships and flags on a light blue background. I had never seen matching wallpaper and bedspreads from where I came from.

Dick then pulled open the drawer of his dresser and said, "Would you like to play Monopoly?" He pulled out the box from the top drawer of his dresser and placed it on the table in the corner that had two chairs with seat cushions that matched the wallpaper.

I said, "I play this with my cousin, Arlene, during the winter months."

Dick then had me sit down as he began setting up the game when his mother called us down for lunch. As we were finishing lunch, the phone rang and his little sister picked up the phone and answered it.

She said a few words and then turned to Dick saying, "It's Monte, and he wants you to come over to play basketball."

She handed the phone to Dick, who then said into the receiver, "Monte. I'm having lunch, but we'll be over in a little bit. I'm bringing Jimmy Brown with me. Is that okay?"

Dick waited for the response and then said, "We'll be over in a little while." Then he hung up the phone and came back to the kitchen table where I was sitting.

He looked straight at me and said, "Hurry up. We're going over to Monte's to play basketball."

It was a typical fall day with overcast skies. We only had to walk down two blocks to get to Monte Kiffin's house. There were five or six boys shooting baskets on Monte's two-car garage concrete driveway. When we arrived, I noticed that all these voices belonged to the same boys we played tag football with at the school playground at lunch time.

Monte said, "Let's play a game of pig until we get enough people here to have a game."

To start the game, Monte threw the ball up towards the basket and it went through the basket rim without touching the rim. We played all afternoon as two teams until it started getting dark. Then everyone started to leave because they had to get back home for supper.

Dick turned to me and said, "Let's go back over to the house, and I'll have my dad drive you home."

I said, "No, I can walk home. It's not that far."

Dick continued playing while I walked the nine blocks home. Basketball at Monte's was played every Saturday and Sunday throughout the football season.

"Stuckey"—as all the boys at school called him—became one of my lifelong friends. Throughout high school, he was a great athlete at track and was at the top of most class activities. He also was a top achiever. He was like a brother to me, and he included me in a lot of activities I would not have experienced otherwise.

In high school, he worked for his dad on their farm, and he took care of their yard in town. We did a lot of things together like going to Lincoln to some of the Cornhusker games and staying in his cousin's room at the dorm for the weekend. He followed me through college and was always someone I could go to for advice and friendship. We always kept in touch even as we became grown men with our own careers and family responsibilities. As a grown man, whenever I went to Denver, my wife and I would always be welcomed into his and his wife's home. He means a lot to me, and I can sincerely say he is my best friend.

Chapter Eight
Freshman Year as an Orphan Boy

When a boy enters high school as a freshman, other students are unaware if he's an orphan. There's nothing about him physically that would set off any alarms. But having grown up in an orphanage, to him, the world looks more like an adventure with all types of new things to learn and experience.

When Jimmy entered Lexington High School as a freshman, he encountered more extracurricular activities than he had ever thought imaginable. He got to be in classes like the boys' glee club, choir, and HI-Y, and he also got to meet new kids at his school, like Roger Sorenson and Roger's older sister, Lila.

I met Roger Sorenson in biology class and learned that his family lived on a large farm in Lexington. One day at the beginning of our lunch hour, Roger approached me at the bike rack and asked me if I would like to ride with him and his sister to Millie's Café for lunch. Roger took me to the parking lot to get in Lila's light blue, four-door 54 Chevy car. At lunchtime, Lila always picked up three or four of her classmates. Roger and I squeezed into the back seat with two other girls. Lila introduced us all and then she drove us to Millie's Café for lunch.

I learned that most farm girls had cars because they lived out on the farm with no transportation to get to high school. Roger would go downtown to get lunch if the Sorenson's forgot to bring their sack lunches. Lunch sacks were not cool in high school. After that first day, Roger and I got to ride with the big girls while driving up and down Washington Street, which was the main street of Lexington at the noon hour.

Roger and I didn't mind squeezing in with the girls in the back seat. We got to hear all the girl talk about who wanted to date who, which boys in high school were cute, along with who was wild and dating who. I loved the smell of their perfume along with watching each of them putting on makeup and lipstick, popping their gum, and combing their hair. It was all part of the noon hour as Roger and I rode around with the girls.

The farm girls stuck together for all their after-school activities. Some of the girls would come by the house, tap the horn, and I would come out and climb in the car. On some days they would take me with them when they had their horse riding classes. I liked being included in their activities, and they were always so nice to me. I was grateful for that.

***

On a typical school day, I would get home somewhere around 5 o'clock, but on this particular day, Grandpa wasn't home yet. I never had any schoolwork to bring home, so I would just sit at the only table we had, which was in the living room. Grandpa had taught me how to play Solitaire and that kept me busy while he was gone. If I wasn't playing cards, I would turn on the radio and sit in Grandpa's big chair listening to Fibber McGee and Mollie. He drove into the driveway about an hour later, got out of the car, and came into the house.

I was sitting in Grandpa's big brown leather chair when he walked in and said, "I'm late because I was out fishing."

I must have had a strange look on my face when he said that, but he didn't see my expression.

He walked through the kitchen to where I was sitting and said, "I have an Odd Fellows meeting to attend tonight, and I don't have time to make dinner, so we're going into town to eat."

We went outside and got in Grandpa's 1949 green Ford sedan. He drove downtown to the café that was around the corner from the Odd Fellows Hall. Millie's Café was in the same building as the town's pool hall. We walked in through the front door of the café and I noticed three people were having their meals. There was a counter that ran the length of the room, which had ten chrome stools covered with red vinyl tops that matched the color of the countertop. That's where Grandpa and I sat down.

A blackboard hung on the back wall of the café where the specials of the day were written in big, white, chalk letters. Behind the counter was a thin, tall man who wore a white apron and a white paper chef's hat. He asked what we wanted to eat.

Grandpa looked at the blackboard on the wall and told the man, "Two meatloaf specials."

As we sat there on the stools, I could see out the windows at the back of the kitchen. There were pool tables in the pool hall where there was some action going on.

I asked Grandpa, "What are they doing back there?"

My guy friends from school never went to the pool hall. They told me it was a place where older boys went, and it was expensive to play. They said they'd rather spend money on candy and drinks.

Grandpa said, "They're playing pool. After dinner, let's go back there and watch them, okay?"

I shook my head and was anxious to eat because I was very hungry, and I liked meatloaf.

After we finished eating, we went down to the front of the pool hall where some high school boys were playing. There were tall chairs along the outside wall where Grandpa and I sat watching the game.

Grandpa said, "The object of this game is to get all the balls in the holes on the table except the white ball called the cue ball and the black eight ball. One player puts all the low numbers while the other puts all the high numbers into the pockets, leaving the eight ball. The eight ball is the last ball to get played, and the winner is the one who gets it in the pocket.

I kept watching the boys play. One after another they were hitting the balls into the holes.

"Grandpa then said, "You can set here and watch, because I have to go to the meeting. You can walk home from here."

"Okay, Grandpa," I told him.

What a Ride

While I was sitting at the pool hall watching the boys finish their game, one of the boys put on his leather jacket and walked in my direction.

He said, "I heard you had to walk home. Would you like to ride with us?" Junior Richards was his name, which I didn't know until later in the evening when everyone called him JR.

The guy following Junior said his name was Dean Brown, and he added, "We'll be happy to give you a ride home. We're getting ready to leave the pool hall."

I said, "Sure," and slid off the tall wooden chair.

I began following Dean out the door and turned to the left. That's when I saw Junior opening the passenger side door of a nice shiny, dark green Chevy coupe. Dean pulled the seat down so I could climb into the back seat of the coupe. It had a light green interior with a pair of red regular dice hanging on his rearview mirror.

As I was climbing into the back seat, I saw that the car had a stick shift on the floor. The gear shift had a black eight ball on the top of the gear shift.

JR got into the driver's side and started the car as Dean Brown sitting in the front passenger seat said, "Let's drag Main Street first to see if there's any action."

I wasn't sure what that meant, so I decided to keep quiet.

As we turned up Main Street, Dean Brown, who was in the passenger's seat, turned to me and said, "What street do you live on, Jimmy?"

"I live at the corner of 8th Street and Lincoln."

Dean then said, "You don't mind riding around a while, Jimmy, do you?"

I told him, "It's okay by me."

We went by the high school past 13th Street and got to the end of Washington Street when we made a U-turn. Then we started to go back down Washington Street. Just as we did, there was another car coming towards us.

Suddenly both cars stopped in the middle of the street.

Dean Brown hollered out his window, "Hey, Dorsey, pull over and climb in with us."

Dean Dorsey, the driver of the other car, said, "Let me park on the side street."

Junior Richards, who was sitting in the driver's seat hollered across Dean Brown, and said, "Park it up by the high school. No one will know the difference."

Just then, Dean Dorsey squealed his tires as he took off going to the end of Washington Street and made a U-turn, like we had just done. Junior Richards started going towards the high school when Dean Dorsey passed him as he tromped on the gas to get in front of our car on our way to the high school, which was only four blocks away.

It was a cold fall evening, and it was getting dark.

Junior Richards said, "Crazy bastard, he's going to wreck his dad's car someday."

As we pulled up into the high school parking lot, Dorsey was already out of his car walking towards us. He opened JR's door and climbed in the back seat with me.

Dean Dorsey looked at me and said, "What the hell is your name? What the hell you doing here?"

Dean Brown turned towards Dean with a slight smirk on his face and said, "Leave him alone. His name is Jimmy Brown. He's a friend of mine, might even be a relative."

Dean Dorsey turned towards Junior Richards, then Junior turned around and looked back to say, "Yeah, we picked him up at the pool hall."

"Hey, twerp," Dorsey hollered, speaking to me, "who do you live with that allows you to be out at night?"

I answered back, "My grandpa lives on 8th Street over by Huff's store."

I had learned a long time ago when Grandpa first brought me to live with him to only answer questions that were directed towards me, because that would help me stay out of trouble.

"Where is your grandpa tonight?"

I answered, "He's up at the Odd Fellows Hall playing pinochle."

Then Dorsey turned to the two up front and said, "Big JR, I want to drive over by the Shell station. I'm supposed to meet Bob to pick up some beer."

Junior then took a hold of the steering knob on his steering wheel and turned it hard to the right while simultaneously stepping on the gas. That made the car spin in a big circle in the middle of the street with smoke coming off the tires. Dean Dorsey came sliding towards me across the back seat, pinning me against the back window as we swung around the circle.

Dean Brown shouted at Junior Richards, "You dumb shit! We're going to get some beer, and you have to let everybody know that we're in town?"

Dean Dorsey pushed himself off me where I was squeezed between the side of the car with heavy Dean against me.

Dean looked down at me who was all crumpled up and said, "Kid, did you get hurt?"

I said, "Not me. That was fun!"

We were now heading towards downtown, and Dean turned left on 3rd Street heading to the Shell station on Highway 30. The car stopped halfway in the block before the Shell station. Dorsey pushed up the front seat where Dean was sitting, got a hold of the door handle, opened the door, got out, and disappeared into the darkness between the two buildings.

Moments later, Dorsey came out of the darkness carrying something in a brown paper bag. He handed the bag to JR as he reached the car, and then he opened the door and climbed into the back seat with me.

In a loud voice, he said, "Let's get the hell out of here before someone sees us."

Again, JR stomps on the gas pedal, spinning the back tires, and lays rubber with a high squealing sound as we take off toward Highway 30 heading out of town.

Dean Brown again says, "Junior, you dumb shit! Why don't you let the whole town know? We've got beer in the car."

Junior Richards turned toward Dean Brown and said, "Shut the hell up and hand me a cigarette."

Then he turned off the first dirt road past the drive-in theater. He all of a sudden slammed on the brakes as he turned out the headlights. The car was still running and the radio was playing rock and roll music from Del Rio, Texas.

I was starting to wonder why we stopped out here with the lights turned off. What is going to happen next?

JR said to Dean, "Give me that cigarette and a light. I have to take a piss."

Then he grabbed a cigarette out of Dean's hand and opened the door by kicking it with his foot. As he hurried to stand outside his front door, he lit the cigarette, and we could all hear the piss hitting the gravel as he stood there with the light of the match reflecting off his round face. He had a short nose between two small piercing eyes overshadowed by heavy dark eyebrows.

Dean Brown slammed his front door shut and poked his head in the window, which was always down. He wanted JR to hear the voom voom sound of the Smitty mufflers he had just put on his car.

Dean looked at JR and asked, "Hey, JR, where is the church key? It's time to have one of those beers, Dino."

JR opened the glove box and started fishing around inside searching for the little metal key. The church key was found and passed back to Dino who still had the brown paper bag between his legs with the beer inside the sack. In a few seconds, I heard a fizzing sound as Dean cut two holes in the top of a can with the church key.

Dino hurried to lift the can up to his mouth to suck the foam that was coming out of the top of the can. At which time Dean mumbled, "Don't you know, damn hot beer."

"I guess I shouldn't have run down the alley with the beer."

He handed the first one to Dean Brown and popped open the second can, and I heard the slurping sound again. He took the foam off the top and then handed that beer to JR, who was still sitting in the front seat, fooling with the radio knobs for music.

He said he was trying to find "Cat Man Jack" the DJ with his rough deep voice coming from Dell Rio, Texas.

Being out here on the flat plains of Nebraska, the radio waves from far away are easier to get on your radio at night.

Dino then pops the third can and hands it to me saying, "Jimmy, you might as well have one since you are a relative of Dean Brown," giving a small fake laugh. "Have you ever drank beer before, Jimmy?"

I said, "No, I haven't. Grandpa doesn't have beer in the house."

Junior said, "Jimmy, go for it. You might like it."

Just then, Dean Brown lets out a long, large burping sound from his mouth after taking two or three big gulps of beer. JR answers with a loud, deep fart, which almost trumps Dean's belch.

Everybody breaks out in laughter, as Dean Dorsey opens the fourth can and says, "JR, something crawled up in your ass and died. God, let me out of this stink hole."

He lunged towards the front to open the door and got out. He turned his back to the car as he started to piss in the weeds on the side of the road.

Junior turned to me and said, "Jimmy, take a drink of that beer. You don't want it to go to waste."

This is when it occurred to me that I was very different from the rest of the guys. I had never even been around anyone who drank. I was taught at the orphanage at our daily morning prayer meeting that if you take one drink of alcohol, you would become a drunkard and go to hell.

I put the can up to my lips and let a mouthful of beer hit my tongue, and then I swallowed the beer. As it went down my throat with all the bubbles, it burnt my throat. All I could think of was that it tasted horrible. To me it tasted like sucking on an old bed sheet that had been dipped in strong cough medicine.

Tears came to my eyes. I was glad I was in the back seat where there were no lights. Then Dean Brown pushed his can of beer into the window as Dino was climbing back into the back seat.

He said, "Let's toast to the first beer that Jimmy Brown has ever drank."

Junior added, "Bring your beer up here."

Then the four of us touched our cans together in a toast. For a moment, I thought this was fun, and maybe I wouldn't go to hell.

Junior said, "Now take a big gulp."

As I did, the second swallow wasn't as bad tasting as the first one that burned my throat. This time I didn't feel such a huge burning sensation. But I could still feel the bubbles going down my throat. By this time, Dean Brown had finished his beer and asked for another one. Dino opened another can, slurped the foam off the can, and handed it to Dean Brown.

Then Dean asked Junior if he was ready for a second one, which he handed to Junior to open.

Do you know, he finished his beer as the three of them were singing a song that came on the radio from Cat Man Jack. He said it was his favorite, "Blue Suede Shoes" by the man Elvis Presley.

Dino turned to me and asked, "How you doing, Jimmy, on that beer?"

He reached over and took the can out of my hand.

"I'll help you kill this thing," he said, taking a drink from it and handing it back to me.

I took another drink and handed it to him, and he finished it.

Again, Junior let out a low, long fart and said, "Try to trump that, boys."

As everybody again broke out in loud laughter, the smell filled the car.

Dean Brown said, "Let's go back to town and see if we can find another contact before the bars close."

Everybody threw their empty beer cans out on the roadside. Dean Brown let out a big, long belch that again brought laughter to all of us in the car. We drove back to town and went up and down Washington Street two or three times with all the windows rolled down and the music playing loudly.

Finally, Junior said, "Stop at the Blue Lounge, and I'll run in to see if I can find Bob or George about getting more beer.

Dean Brown then said, "It's 11:30, and we better take Jimmy home before he gets into trouble. Where do you live, Jimmy?"

"On 8th Street over by Huffs Stop & Shop."

Junior turned the car around and drove me to my house.

Dean Dorsey said, "How are you feeling, Jimmy?"

I said, "I feel alright, although my head feels light."

"Okay, we'll see you tomorrow at school."

I got out of his car and Dean closed the passenger door. The three of them took off, and I turned to go into the house. I didn't know if grandpa was home or not because he always parked his car in the garage. As I walked into the front door of the house, the only light I saw was coming from the bedroom where the bedside table held the bronze lady lamp. She had a fancy shape and she had her right arm holding up the lamp shade. As I took off my shirt, shoes, and pants, I saw that Grandpa was in bed asleep. I crawled over him very lightly which I had done two or three other times when I got home late from running with the gang. I got on the inside of the bed. Then I climbed underneath the goose down blanket with a smile on my face, happy to have had so many fun times with my friends.

Chapter Nine
Working at the Ballpark

After school and on weekends, I was spending a lot of my time with the guys. We'd go downtown and wait outside of a bar for Bill Montoya to run inside the bar to get some money from his dad or uncle, so we could buy ice cream, etc. One evening, Monte and Bill knocked on my front door. They told me to get on my bike because they would take me out to the fairgrounds to work at the ballpark.

The fairgrounds was on the south side of the track and it took us twenty minutes to get there. When we approached the fairgrounds, it was getting dark but they had bright lights over the baseball field. The three of us rode our bikes to the concession stand. Bill got off his bike, and then we went in the side door to talk to the head man running the stand.

The man followed Bill out the side door and said to me, "Would you be willing to work tonight to sell soda pop?"

I asked, "What do I have to do to get started?"

Bill introduced me to a man called "Mr. Gus."

Mr. Gus said, "Bill and Monte will show you what you have to do this evening."

He explained to me that he would give me two dollars in change, and then they handed me a small apron that I wrapped around my waist with the change in it. I was to sell soda pop at $.15 each. Meanwhile, Bill was getting a soda pop box made out of wood that had twenty-four small squares in the bottom to hold the bottles of Coke, Pepsi, and other sodas. Then Bill hooked one end of a wide strap around one end of the box and placed the strap across my back, around my neck, and then around the other end of the box.

Monte then took me over to the cooler and placed ten bottles of different brands of soda pop into the box. I couldn't carry anymore for the weight would be too heavy for me. I then had to sell the ten bottles of pop. When I had sold all ten bottles, I returned to the concession stand and gave Mr. Gus $1.50 that I had made on selling soda pop.

Monte then loaded my box up to take out into the stands. Monte said I should howler, "Ice Cold Pop" as I went up and down the aisles of the bleachers. I got a lot of sales because all the ladies would stop to ask me questions because I was the littlest kid selling soda pop. I would go home with anywhere from three to seven dollars in tips along with two dollars for labor.

One evening while I was selling soda pop, a foul ball came whirling into the stands. The ball hit the top of the bleachers and the ball fell down right in front of me. I happened to be standing there and picked up the ball. Three other young boys came to get the ball. One of the kids that was chasing the ball told me I should go down on the field to talk to Steve. I was on my last bottle of soda to sell so I went down to find Steve. He was the only big kid who had a baseball glove telling everybody what to do. I approached Steve.

He said, "You got the ball that came into the stands?"

"Yes," I said.

He held out his hand with a quarter in it, and said, "I'll give you this for the ball."

I knew him from somewhere but couldn't place him. He handed me the quarter.

Steve then asked me what my name was as he told me his name was Steve Smith. He said, "I'm in charge of the foul balls for these night games."

He had a glove on and stood in back of home base where most of the foul balls came. Then I remembered last year, Terry, my cousin, took me to the Lexington town team for he was asked to play shortstop for the team. I already had a baseball outfit since I was the bat boy for the Overton Junior Legion team. That was because Terry was playing on their team last year, and I went to all the practices.

When the coach asked me to be the bat boy, Terry and I looked through the pages of the Sears and Roebuck's catalog and found a baseball outfit for me to wear. The coach told me the things I had to do. The most important thing was to run out and pick up the bat as soon as the batter let go of it, regardless if the batter ran the bases or struck out.

Terry took me to his first practice with the Lexington town team and told me to sit on the bench until practice was over. I was already wearing my baseball hat and outfit. The boys were having batting practice and running to first base. I had nothing to do, so as soon as the batter let go of his bat, I ran out, picked up the bat, and placed it into the bat rack. I felt that I was helping the coach. After about the fifth batter, I had this kid who was around my age but taller and well-built come over to me. He grabbed the front of my baseball shirt and pulled me up to his face so he could look directly in my eyes.

He said, "What do you think you're doing?"

The words seemed to squeak out of my throat, "I was being the bat boy."

He let go of my shirt and I had to catch my balance as my feet searched for firm ground to stand on.

He wailed at me, "I'm Steve. I'm the bat boy. My dad is the coach. Now don't run so fast after the bats."

I tried not to roll my eyes but my brain was wondering why he would even say that. Did he want me to run slow to pick up the bats? It didn't make any sense.

Steve said, "I'll allow you to help me. You can chase down every other bat today, but don't run so fast. Next practice, I'll be the bat boy."

I asked him, "Didn't I meet you as a bat boy for this home team last year?"

Steve said, "Yes, I remember you. You little shit. You almost took my job."

I then said, "Here, you can have this last Orange Crush. I'll pay for it."

I turned and went back to the concession stand to load up again with more than ten bottles.

I liked selling pop because their family was nice to me. Mr. Gus was also nice and told me I was doing a good job selling pop. By the end of the night after going under the stands and on top of the stands to find empty bottles, I got on my bike and arrived at Grandpa's around 11:45 p.m. Grandpa was asleep in the bed.

As I laid awake in bed looking at the stars outside the bedroom window, I was feeling grateful for everyone in my life, especially Grandpa. He never questioned where I had been or what time I got home. It's like he had this invisible confidence in me, and I felt content knowing I was loved and trusted.

Chapter Ten

Sophomore Year Transportation and Jobs

My means of transportation was a bike that Grandpa had bought for me when I was living in the orphanage. I was nine years old at the time. Now as a sophomore and living with Grandpa, if I would sometimes leave my bike on someone's sidewalk or lawn to go somewhere to play, it would always be right in the same spot where I had left it.

My bike was small, red and white, and it had red fenders. I thought it was so cool, that is, until I saw Tom Sheldon's blue bike with handle bars inverted that stuck up in the air instead of down. He had his front fender cut off at the top. I was envious. He had the back fender chopped off halfway up from the back. The other thing he did was raise his seat as high as he could get it. He had long legs anyway so he looked so cool riding his bike when he was in junior high school. I took my little twenty-four-inch bike, cut my fenders, raised my seat, and then repainted my bike red with white trim. I was glad Grandpa had a lot of tools in his shed I could use to alter my bike.

When Tom got to the age of driving, his mom allowed him to buy a white Chevy coup. That's when he sold me his blue bike, and I really thought I was hot (meaning I loved that bike and the way it looked). He had the cutest girls in school attracted to him. He was a talented athlete and he knew it. He got his car customized at the local Chevy garage. Tom had it lowered in the back with all the chrome taken off with smooth curved fender skirts over the back wheel well also along with little red taillights with the back wide chrome bumper. It had "Smitty "mufflers which would make it purr when cruising down Washington Street.

Tom lived with his mother in a modest house on Washington Street and he didn't have a dad because of a divorce when he was in grade school. He must have related to my style of life because he would drag me around with him in his Chevy when he was in high school. He was always the center of attention wherever he went. I knew he had a soft heart but no one else did, because he wouldn't show it. He knew how to keep feelings close to the chest. I learned a lot from him. He was someone to watch.

Everything Isn't Always the Way It Appears

During the summer of my sophomore year in high school, I was fifteen and I wanted to earn some spending money. At that time, I didn't know what I could do, but I knew I enjoyed exploring new things around our town.

A bunch of us kids had heard that a carnival was coming to our city for the County Fair which was held each year at the fairgrounds. So we went to watch the carnival crew set up the rides and the side games. I asked one of the workers where I could go to get a job. He pointed to a small dirty trailer in back of the freak show tent.

"Ask for Frank," he told me.

I went over, climbed the three steps, and then tapped on the door of the trailer. After the second knock, a grouchy male voice yelled, "Come in."

When I opened the door to climb into the trailer, I saw a little old man sitting at a wide desk. He had a stogie in his mouth and was holding a phone to his ear. He had a dirty old somewhat white sea captain cap on his sweaty head. He had sweat stains on his shirt under his arms along with holes in his blue shirt. He had his sleeves rolled up to his elbows and was giving someone hell on the phone.

He hung up, turned to me, and with a gravely voice, said, "What do you want?"

"One of the guys outside told me to come in and ask to see Frank."

"Yeah, so what?" he blared.

"I would like a job," I said in my most confident voice.

He looked at me, then asked, "How old are you?"

"Fifteen."

He said, "Could you come back tomorrow at 10 o'clock? By then I'll know if I have something available."

I nodded, and hurried out the door.

***

The next day I showed up at the fairgrounds around 8 o'clock to watch the crew put up the big tent. At 9:30 I saw the little old man, Frank, and I ran to stop him.

"You said you wanted to see me at 10 o'clock today about the job."

He said, "Follow me."

So I followed him to a little booth located next to the Ferris wheel with the octopus ride on the other side of the small booth. He opened the door to the booth.

"Sit in this chair and sell tickets to these two rides."

I looked at the cramped area behind the window and the small chair. I wondered how I would be able to handle this small cramped space all day.

He said, "I will be right back." Then he closed the door.

About fifteen minutes later he came back with his hands full of different things. He placed a tin box on the counter and opened the box which had different quantities of change.

He said, "There's sixty dollars in the box. If you need more change, I'll be around throughout the day."

He than gave me a big roll of tickets and told me to sell each ticket for thirty-five cents apiece or three for one dollar. Next, he taped a cardboard sign outside of the glass. The sign listed the prices of the tickets I was to sell. Then he left me sitting there.

A roughnecked guy came to the booth door and pounded on it. The vibration shook the entire booth, and it scared the shit out of me. Here I was sitting with sixty dollars, which I had never seen before along with some big burley guy who was banging on the door to my booth.

Frank had told me before he left me with the tickets and the money, "Don't let anyone in the door. Keep it locked at all times."

The guy banging on the door was inpatient. He came around to the front window and said, "I'm starting the Ferris wheel, so start selling tickets."

I had about ten people lining up outside the window. I must have sold 400 tickets before noon. I had a lot of money in piles on the floor and on the counter where my cash box was placed. I had to pee so bad that I thought I would have to just pee my pants and not tell anyone because they couldn't see under the counter where I sat.

Finally Frank came to the window and asked me what the number on the first ticket was that I had to sell. Of course I did not know the number for no one told me to write the number down. He then asked if I needed any change. I told him I didn't have any quarters. He told me to give him ten dollars and then he ran off. I kept on selling tickets until he came back with rolls of quarters. By this time I was dancing in the booth because I had to pee so bad. I was trying to sell tickets with one hand which was a hard thing to do. I had only one hand because the other hand was squeezing my pecker from peeing my pants.

When I saw Frank, I yelled out to him, "Can you help me? I have to pee."

He looked at me as if I wasn't there. Then he said, "Oh, I forgot about that fact."

He came to the door. I unlocked it. Then I rushed out to find the closest bathroom, which was behind the cotton candy booth.

After I had emptied my bladder, I headed back to the booth. Frank opened the door and left. I sat back down on the stool again and kept selling tickets until around 3 o'clock when Frank came by asking me to put all the big bills I had in the booth into the sack he handed me.

Of course I was too dumb to put the number of the first ticket I sold so I could compare it to the number I had now. He told me to keep one hundred dollars of the change I had in the tin box. I must have sold another 600 tickets, because I had a lot of money in that little booth at 5 o'clock.

Frank came by and let me out to pee again. He gave me a dollar and told me to get a hotdog, which I did on my way back to the booth. My back started to hurt around 8 o'clock from going from standing to sitting on the tall stool which was in the booth. Frank came around again to pick up the extra money I had in the booth but he forgot to give me a pee break. I sold tickets until 11 o'clock that evening. Frank came by the booth, took all the money and tickets with him, along with the tin box.

He said, "Son, follow me. It's closing time."

I had to run out of the little booth to catch him as he scooted to the trailer. I told him I really had to pee. He directed me to the toilet which was a great relief. As I came out of the toilet Frank told me to sit down. It felt so good to sit in a normal chair. I was exhausted. He went to the back of the desk and then started counting my money from the bag I gave him around noon today. Also he had the money we had just taken out of the booth. He looked at all the tickets I had left which was only a little roll. I must have sold 1,200 tickets the way I felt sitting there in this nice chair. I didn't have any slow times in front of my booth. I had a line of people always waiting to buy tickets.

After a while Frank looked up from the desk. Then he said, "Son, after looking at the numbers, your count is off by forty dollars."

This made no sense to me as I sat there dog tired, hungry, and sweating from being in that booth all day. The temperature must have been 100 degrees with the sun beating down on the booth with no ventilation.

Frank continued saying, "Son, I can't pay you because of this loss and don't come back tomorrow."

He stood up and came around the desk with his arms stretched, like indicating I should head for the door because he was on his way out to pick up another sucker.

This was my first experience of someone who took advantage of "greenhorns" who trust every word that is spoken as the truth. This is what I was taught in the church during our lectures in morning chapel at the orphanage.

I went home to Grandpa that night climbing over him to get in the feather bed. It had been an extremely long day. The next morning I told him about my all-day job with no pay. He listened to my story.

Then he said, "Yesterday, you learned there are people in this world who will take advantage of you. So consider the source of some people but do not trust those carnies people. End of lesson.

After that day, I thought to myself that as you go through life, you will sometimes make the wrong decision. Every person that I have talked to has made mistakes if you ask them about it. Mistakes are good. You should welcome them if you have learned from that mistake.

Chapter Eleven
Taming My Hormones

Mylan Phelps, the guy I met during one of our touch football games, delighted in talking to me about our tenth grade English teacher. She was a turn on for both of us. She was a nice looking lady about forty or so years old, and she had big boobs. She wore a lot of tight suits, and when she walked down the aisle in class, I could hear a sound of something nylon rubbing together. My mind would go wild hearing this sound, and that's when my sex hormones would kick in. I couldn't imagine what that sound was coming from. I finally asked Mylan, and he said it was her nylons rubbing against the top of her thighs. What a turn on. I imagined seeing this in action without a skirt on this lady. This is where my *nooner* started to take over my body until I graduated from college. To me, a nooner is what happened to my body every day around 12 o'clock. I would get a hard on that lasted for twenty minutes and then it would disappear. I had no one to talk to about this. Certainly, I couldn't say anything to Grandpa.

My hormones were out of control but I got turned on every day in English class. After class one day, Mylan and I approached our teacher and we asked her if she would like to go to dinner with the two of us some evening. She agreed to a time and a day. I don't know how Mylan got out of dinner with his family, but I told Grandpa that I was eating over at someone's house, which was a common occurrence for me.

Mylan and I talked about how we would put the moves on this teacher. We wanted to see where this sound was coming from and maybe see some boobs. We both talked a long time about how huge her boobs looked. In fact, that's what we talked about every afternoon after class. We met with her at the high school around 6 o'clock. We got in her car and went to a local restaurant. I sat across from Mylan and he got to sit beside her. I wanted Mylan to put his hand on her thigh under the table.

I had discussed this with him the night before while we were considering tactics for how to get her hot-hot-hot. I kicked Mylan under the table but he didn't know what to say, so we carried on a non-sexual conversation. I tried by asking questions such as, "How many children do you have? Where is your husband? Do you have a boyfriend?" Statements such as, "You have nice clothing. Where do you buy your clothes you wear in school?" I thought maybe I could find her buying her underwear some day and help her pick it out.

We found out where she lived, which was above the movie theater in an apartment. At the end of the meal, we were going to pay for the bill but she insisted on paying and wouldn't let us pay. She then said she had papers to grade and took us back to the school. She told us she enjoyed the company. Mylan and I got on our bikes and rode back downtown to the back of her apartment building. We went into the hallway and found her mailbox with the number of her apartment. Then we went upstairs and found her door. We counted the doors to the end of the hall. Then we went outside and counted the windows from the end of the building to identify the windows of her apartment.

There was a one-story dentist's office in the back of her apartment, where we climbed on top of the garbage bin, and then pulled ourselves up to the top of that building. The building was flat on the top so we could sit up against the building on the roof and observe the windows that belonged to our lady. We must have stayed up there two or three hours that evening watching her apartment window hoping to get a glimpse of her undressing. We wanted to see those big boobs so bad.

For the rest of that week we lived on the roof of the dentist's office every evening when we could get out of the house. We never did get to see any skin. In our dreams and conversations, we saw a lot of big boobs and a great body that belonged to our teacher. I still can hear the silky swishing sound of her nylons as she walked down the aisle during our English class just before our lunch hour. I listened to her walking every day until the end of the school semester. Mylan moved on to football, and I moved on to other erotic situations, like looking at Dick Stuckey's *Playboy* magazine that he got from his job at Jack and Jill's grocery store.

Chapter Twelve

Junior Year Surprises and New Car Escapades

During my junior year of high school, I worked for Lyman Stuckey, father of my classmate, Dick, who lived in a big house at the end of town. Dick and I helped Lyman fix his barn, and I mowed the lawn and did all the odd jobs he needed done. On other days, I would go to Bud Breck's house, another classmate who had a house on Stuckey's farm. I helped Bud with gardening chores and other projects Lyman needed done.

Everything was going along as usual until one autumn afternoon. Lyman wanted me and his son, Dick, to go out to the farm and burn off the dry weeds in his irrigation ditches that had grown there throughout the summer months. So early one fall Saturday morning, we drove out to the farm. I noticed that Dick had brought gas cans full of tractor fuel with him to burn the weeds out of the irrigation ditches. Lyman had told Dick he wanted us to go along the top side of the ditches and pour gas on both sides of the ditch. So that's exactly what we did. The sloped ditches measured about five feet deep and four feet across. Dick instructed me to stand back while he lit a match and threw it onto the tractor fuel we had scattered in the ditch.

The first time we did this, I was awestruck at the sight of those weeds going up in flames so fast. All I could hear was a whooshing sound as the flames of fire burned in a path. Dick then brought out a pack of Marlboro cigarettes.

He told me, "Here, light up and we can get this job done much faster and not waste matches."

This was the first time I knew that Dick smoked. We could burn only so much at a time because we had to control the fire. We'd stand at the next patch of dry weeds and see that everything behind us was black that we had burned previously.

As the day went on, we challenged each other to see if we could get the fire to make that whooshing noise when we lit the tractor fuel with the tip of our burning cigarette in the next patch of weeds. By this time, we were breaking off stems of the dried weed and lighting the tips with the existing fire. Then we'd run to the next group of weeds to hear that whooshing noise.

Dick got caught down inside the ditch once as I torched the next group of weeds. He came out of the ditch with all of his eyebrows singed off. He dared me to see if I could get to the other side of the ditch on the next burn. He started the whoosh burn at the same time I started running towards the ditch. Then I ran down the side of the ditch, across the bottom of the ditch, and then back up the other side while the fire was spreading fast around me.

Dick said he couldn't see me for maybe thirty seconds because the flames were so high. He said later he didn't think I would make it. What we had done was button down our sleeves, pulled down our stocking caps over our hair where we both had glasses on to protect our eyes. We wore big boots along with blue jeans that helped protect our legs. We did this about two or three times before it got too dark.

We both had no eyebrows that night at supper, but we didn't tell Mrs. Stuckey how that happened. Dick and I did a lot of marginal things as we went through our high school years. He is my kind of guy!!!

***

My whole life has been a risk on my part. The Guardian Angel who was assigned to take care of Jimmy Brown had a big job on her hands. If I was to meet her, before I got married, I could only imagine what she looked like. Her feathers would be out of alignment with two or three feathers missing. Her halo would be all bent out of shape, the luster gone, and her halo would be tipped to one side of her head along with her hair all frizzed out. She would have a couple of fingernails bitten down to the nubs. Her effort to keep me out of harm's way was more than a full-time job.

Buying My First Car

In the spring of 1956, I bought a 1949 Ford coupe from Tom Sheldon because Tom had advanced to a 1954 Chevy coupe. He was having the car customized at the local Chevy auto shop. I drove my car to school the day after I got my driver's license. At lunchtime, Roger Sorensen rode with me to Millie's Café.

Roger asked, "Are you going to do something with this car?"

I said, "What should I be doing to this car? I already have fender skirts and whitewall tires on all four wheels."

He said, "What about lowering the back of the car and taking all the chrome off your hood and sides? Then you could get moon hubcaps for all four wheels."

Tom Sheldon had already put fender skirts on this car. He also switched the steering wheel gearshift to the opposite side. That meant I had to learn to shift backwards. Tom also put on new seat covers to match the interior of the car.

I then turned to Roger and said, "Do you know how to do all this customization work?"

Roger said, "It's not that hard. All you have to do is get some metal putty and take the chrome off. That will leave holes in the side of your car. You then take the metal putty and put it in the holes and let it dry. Then you use sandpaper to sand it down so it's smooth. That could be the first thing we do to your car to customize it and make it yours.

I thanked Roger for his suggestion and told him I'd think about it and talk to Tom Sheldon.

When I saw Tom later that evening, I told him what Roger had suggested.

Tom said, "I can ask the guy who is customizing my car if he could get us the metal putty from the auto shop."

"Great," said Jimmy.

I saw Tom the next day and he told me, "The shop guy wants twenty dollars for the metal putty can. It would give you enough to cover all the holes where the chrome was on your car."

I gave Tom twenty dollars, and the next day he gave me a can of metal putty along with a packet of sandpaper, courtesy of the mechanic at the Chevy dealer.

Tom said, "The guy at the Chevy auto shop paints cars on the side in the garage at his house. So when you get finished sanding everything, you'll want your car painted. He's willing to do it at his house for a lower fee."

The following Saturday Roger came over and brought a toolbox with him. The first thing he did was take out a screwdriver and showed me how to pop the chrome clips out of the metal on the hood of my car.

Roger handed me the screwdriver and said, "Go ahead. Start popping off the chrome strips. I'll take a putty knife and start putting putty in the holes that you leave."

"Okay, thanks," I said.

"Roger quickly reminded me, "We have to let this putty harden and dry for twenty-four hours before we can start sanding."

"How long do you think it will take me to get all these strips of chrome off?"

"I don't know. Three or four hours. But if it's any incentive, my sister will be finished with her horse classes at the fairgrounds around noon, and that's when she's picking me up," Roger said, smiling as if challenging me.

"Well then," Jimmy said, "I'd better get moving."

By 12 o'clock, Jimmy had all the strips of chrome taken off the hood, the side doors, and the trunk. Roger worked diligently getting the metal putty into the holes, and he finished before his sister, Lila, showed up to drive him back to his home on the farm.

The next Saturday Roger showed up in the morning at Jimmy's house. He had a bumper jack with him so we could jack up the back of the car to the point where the back wheels were off the ground. We put a block of wood in front of each of the front tires so the car wouldn't roll forward.

Then Roger and I took off the rear tires. Roger climbed underneath the car and began taking the back springs off. The springs had an upward curve that made the car ride softer when it rode over large bumps in the road. Roger then turned the springs upside down and replaced the springs on the frame of the car. This lowered the back bumper of the car to maybe six inches off the ground.

Roger looked at Jimmy and said, "We need to get the bumper to maybe four inches off the ground. Do you have anything heavy that we could put in the trunk to lower the back of the car?"

I said, "Grandpa has some concrete blocks in his work shed."

We quickly placed two of the thirty-pound concrete blocks in the trunk. The back bumper of the car was maybe four inches off the ground after adding the extra weight. Then we started to sand some of the holes that were filled with the dried metal putty. Roger helped until his sister drove up to the front of the house, and then he had to leave.

***

The next week we had Friday off from school, so Roger came over and we worked all day Friday sanding the car to make everything smooth. After that was done, we sat down and looked through the "JC Whitney" auto accessory catalog for moon hubcaps. We found just the right ones for twenty-six dollars each.

I asked Tom Sheldon to set up a time for us to drive over to his friend's garage to see about getting the car painted. The guy wanted $120 to paint my car a dark blue. It took him approximately two weeks to get the car painted. I was glad I had saved all my money from working odd jobs for people so I could pay to have my car painted. But

I had to wait another two weeks to find the money to pay for the moon hubcaps.

To make that extra money, I would pick up boys who wanted a ride to school in the morning. I charged them fifty cents a week. I'd buy one or two dollars' worth of gas, which was four gallons per dollar. Before then I never could fill up the tank because I didn't have that kind of money.

It wasn't too long until I was riding around town with the moon hubcaps on and the lowered car. I thought I looked cool driving around town as a junior in high school. To my surprise, I found out that the moon hubcaps on the front wheels would come off if I turned a corner too fast, like the time when I drove past Sally Lancaster's house.

Sally was the daughter of Logan Lancaster, and they lived on the corner of 17th Street. Just for fun I would try to get my speed up as I approached their corner. I'd make a sharp right turn, and sure enough, my right front hubcap would fly off and go spinning up over the curb, then across their lawn, and it finally bounced up on the two steps of their porch. My goal was to get the hubcap up on their porch. I did it a couple of times. But unfortunately, one time Logan Lancaster was home, and he caught me coming up to his porch to retrieve the hubcap. Logan told me not to do that again. Maybe I forgot to mention it, but Logan Lancaster was the driver's ed teacher at the high school when I took his driver's Ed course to qualify for my driver's license.

Chapter Thirteen
The End of My World

One morning when Grandpa was eighty-three years old, he woke me up at 6:30 a.m., which wasn't a normal hour for him to be awake. He had a panic sound in his voice. He told me to call the ambulance because he had been up in the middle of the night trying to get rid of food that was stuck in his throat. He was having a hard time swallowing and breathing.

Sometimes he would try to dislodge the food with drinking water before he could continue to eat. This was happening once every two months but until now, he was controlling the problem.

I called the ambulance and not long after placing the call, the ambulance got to the house.

While they were putting grandpa on the gurney, he said to me, "Jimmy, you go on to school for I will be all right. I will be home when you get out of school."

When I got home for lunch, Aunt Thelma was at grandpa's. She told me that grandpa was in the hospital doing tests. She was taking me to the hospital to have lunch with her in the kitchen. She worked there as the head cook. She told me she would feed me, and then she'd take me up to grandpa's room.

While having lunch with Aunt Thelma, she said, "Don't be scared but grandpa had a heart attack."

I couldn't even say anything. I was so shocked. I waited to hear what Aunt Thelma would say next.

"I want to take you upstairs to see him. Grandpa told me to tell you not to worry because he would be home in a couple of days."

We went upstairs to the hospital's third floor. When we found his room, he was the only one in the room. There were no other beds besides his. He was sitting up in the bed with pillows all around him.

He asked me, "How is school going this morning?"

I told him, "I'm going to be in a school play. They picked me this morning to be in 'Arsenic and Old Lace.'"

He said, "I am feeling very tired at the moment, so you go on to school."

I wanted to honor his wishes, and I truly believed he would be back at the house in a couple of days.

I then bent over him to get a hold of his neck and I gave him a hug.

After that, I turned towards Aunt Thelma, and said, "I can walk. It's only six blocks from the hospital to school."

Before I left, Aunt Thelma suggested that I stay with her for a couple of days while Grandpa was in the hospital. She said she could take me to school in the morning, and it would still give her enough time to get to her job at the hospital. She said she'd pick me up from school around 4 o'clock when she got off work. I told her I had play practice every night, besides I had to take care of Mrs. Dienfenbach's animal every evening.

"Are you sure you'll do okay being in your house alone without Grandpa there?" she asked.

"I'll be fine. And I'll see you everyday when I come to the hospital to see Grandpa and have lunch with you."

Aunt Thelma looked at me like she was thinking if she should let me do this on my own. "Okay," she finally said, "but don't hesitate if you want to stay at my house instead."

I thanked her for being so kind to think about me, but I was old enough to stay home by myself if it was only for a couple days. I would be busy and come to the hospital to have lunch with her every day, which would also give me a chance to visit with Grandpa.

***

Being at home the next two days without Grandpa felt quite strange, although I knew I was cared for because Aunt Thelma brought me plates of food for my supper.

I missed Grandpa, especially at night, because the house was so quiet. I would climb in the bed and say a little prayer for him to get better and come home soon.

The next two days I left school a little before noon so I could eat lunch at the hospital with Aunt Thelma, and then we'd both go see Grandpa in his room.

I still worked for Mrs. Dienfenbach after school, taking care of her animals. But on the next Saturday while raking leaves in her front yard, Mrs. Stuckey drove up in front of the house. She stopped her car and rolled down the passenger window.

She leaned towards me and said, "I just heard about your grandpa being in the hospital. You should come up to our house and stay with my son, Dick, until your grandpa gets home from the hospital."

I said, "Thank you, but I think Grandpa's coming home soon."

That afternoon, Aunt Thelma called me at Mary Dienfenbach's house. Mary told Aunt Thelma that I was raking leaves across the street for her sister, Susan, who had MS for the past four years and was unable to stand or transfer out of her wheelchair.

"Thelma," Mary said, "I'll holler for Jimmy to come inside, and then you can speak to him."

"Thank you, Mary."

I walked inside Mary's front door and she motioned for me to take the phone.

"It's your Aunt Thelma," she said.

"Hi. This is Jimmy," I announced into the phone.

"Jimmy," Aunt Thelma said with a sadness in her voice, "Grandpa died and went to heaven this afternoon. I need you to go back home and wait there for me, okay?"

I didn't know what to say. Grandpa died? But he said he'd be home in a couple days. Hearing that news on the phone felt paralyzing to me. I felt like I couldn't move.

"Jimmy?" I heard Aunt Thelma say through the phone's speaker. "Are you there?"

"Yes, I'm here. I can't believe what you just told me. What am I supposed to do now?"

"Go back to Susan's house and tell her you will finish raking the leaves another day. I'm leaving the hospital in a little bit and then I'll meet you at home, okay?"

I hung up the phone and thanked Mary for coming to get me.

"I'm so sorry," Mary said.

I walked out the front door and couldn't even look at her, let alone respond to what she had said.

Across the street, Susan's housekeeper was waiting for me at the door. Susan was hanging up the telephone for Mary had called her with the news.

Susan was sitting in her wheelchair and held out her arms, welcoming me.

"Come and sit down for a minute, Jimmy."

I sat down on the sofa as if in a fog and like someone had stolen my brain. *What just happened?* Thoughts inside my head were spinning, and I couldn't even control the crazy emotions I was feeling.

Susan wheeled closer to me and offered me to take her hands, so I did.

"Jimmy, I have some advice for you, and I'm going to tell you what's going to happen in the next few days."

I could barely even look at her, but I knew she cared or she wouldn't be talking to me right now.

She told me, "Jimmy, you need to go home, lie down on the bed, and cry your eyes out. Seriously! You're going to feel a lot of hard, deep down pain about losing Grandpa. Just let your feelings out. Just scream and stomp and holler as loud as you want. Do it! No one will be around to see you or hear you. This is YOUR time to let your emotions out and not keep everything bottled up inside you. Do you understand?"

I said, "Yes, thank you for caring about me."

Then I got up to leave.

Susan said, "If you do this, you'll be able to get through the funeral as well as other things that will take place in the next couple of days."

As I rode my bike back to Grandpa's, I started to cry. By the time I got to the house, I was bawling out loud.

I stormed in through the front door and ran to the bedroom. I threw myself down on Grandpa's bed. Again, tears and wails of hurt and angry words turned to bawling out loud for the next two hours. No one else was there, and I didn't have to worry about anyone finding me in this sad and pitiful state of feeling abandoned once again.

I was bawling for the loss of him leaving and for taking his love with him. Now the only thing I had of my past to love was my dog, Nickie. He was someone I could hold and kiss and hug. I never had anyone to hug and kiss except for the big girls at the orphanage when I was three years old. They hugged me and carried me around when I was three years old. Grandpa left me at the orphanage without letting me know he was leaving. To this day, I cannot say goodbye to anyone because the feelings of abandonment are too deep.

I thought about when I was growing up how much I didn't like to be hugged or have someone touch any part of my skin. Because everyone I cared about would leave me. Susie's advice was very important for helping me deal with my anger and pain.

Thank God for Uncles

After the funeral, Terry, Aunt Thelma's son, whom I lived with on the farm in Overton every summer, was like a brother to me. He lived in Kansas City, so during the Christmas holiday, he took me there to spend time with his two roommates. I didn't know where I would be living when I got back to Lexington.

Going to Kansas City with Terry was to keep me busy until some decisions could be made. When I got back to Lexington, Uncle Don was at Grandpa's house. He was the executor of Grandpa's estate. Terry and I had driven to Grandpa's house where we met with Don. At that time, Uncle Don told me that he had to put my dog Nickie to sleep because of Nickie's health. He could no longer hold his bladder, and he was also having troubles walking because of the pain in his hips.

Really? I thought. *Really? Even Nickie died?*

After I sighed a lot and walked outside to regain my composure, I heard Uncle Don talking to Terry and Aunt Thelma about what they should do next. But I couldn't listen to any of it. I was too devastated that Nickie wasn't here anymore either. Tears streamed down my cheeks as I thought, *I didn't even get to say goodbye to him, and now I'll never see him again.*

A few minutes later, Terry stuck his head out the front door and said, "Jimmy, please come in here. We have something to tell you."

I walked back inside, but I didn't have a feeling like I was going to get good news.

Uncle Don said, "Join us," as he pointed to a chair at the kitchen table.

I sat down and now the three of them were sitting at the table with me and everyone was staring at me.

Uncle Don said, "Ella and I have decided that we would like you to move to our house to finish your junior and senior year of high school.

I will be selling Grandpa's house as soon as we clear out the furniture and his belongings."

I don't know that I was ready for that news, but I was grateful they had made a plan for me and weren't going to leave me somewhere without them.

"What about all my things?" I asked Uncle Don. "And what about the things I want to have that meant something to me from Grandpa?"

Then Uncle Don said, "Jimmy, you will come back here with me next week, and we will pick up all the things you want to bring over to our house. Everything you want. Absolutely everything. Are you okay with the idea of coming to live with us?"

I said, "I guess it will be okay, because I have no other place to stay."

In my heart I was smiling because uncle Don was one of my favorite uncles. And I have always had fun with his son, Tim, who was two years younger than I was. In a way, I was relieved to know something about my future, but it was still one of the most difficult days I can remember in my life.

***

I lived with Uncle Don, Aunt Ella, and their son, Tim, during my last year as a junior in high school. Lucky for me, they added an upstairs bedroom onto their house. This is where Tim and myself had our own kingdom. Tim had a great collection of 33 rpm records with a great record player. I had my gun collection that hung on the gun rack I made in shop class during the first semester of my junior year.

I had never lived with rules and regulations during all the time I had lived with Grandpa. That meant since I was living with a new family, I had to learn how to live by their household rules to keep things on the level. One of the first rules was showing up for dinner at 5:00. I couldn't keep Ella waiting from serving dinner. My only other choice was to tell her in advance if I was going somewhere or if I had other plans. I also had to call Ella and let her know if I was going to be out late with the boys or at class plays. She would not sleep until I got in the house. She said she would worry about me. No one ever told me that before.

As the days went on, my friends from school got into the habit of meeting at Don and Ella's after school instead of meeting at Stuart's Drugs. We would all watch our favorite program in the afternoon—"Dick Clark's American Bandstand." Our group of school kids consisted of girls and guys who were not into sports after football season. Of course, the girls and some guys had to smoke and dirty up the house with smoke. Then after they would leave, I had to open the windows to get the smell out of the house.

To make everyone accountable, I had the group clean up the ashtrays as well as tidy up the house. This lasted for three or four weeks. Then Ella sat down with me one evening while I was eating dinner.

She said, "Which one of your friends was smoking in my house?"

Ella was at work while our group was watching "American Bandstand," and I didn't think Ella even knew we were partying in her house.

I told her, "We come over after school to watch 'American Bandstand,' and then we straighten everything up and get rid of the cigarette butts."

She said, "I don't mind them being here, but if they want to smoke and still be able to come to this house, they will have to smoke outside."

Well, once I informed the group about the new rule, they stopped coming over. Soon after, we found another home where we could meet after school.

***

I really learned a lot about how to treat the woman of the house, because Ella is the one who does most of the work to keep a house clean and neat. The nice little things in a house are there because this lady makes it that way with a lot of work and planning. Most boys I went home with didn't understand that fact, because they had never thought about it while they were growing up.

I learned to quickly appreciate how much effort working mothers put into making a home for their family. I don't know if fathers sit down with their sons to tell them how to handle situations where mothers are involved. Fathers who miss this part of communicating with their sons are the ones who need to understand how to keep things in perspective. Mothers are the greatest factor of families. They are my kind of people.

Chapter Fourteen

Playing in Army Tanks Leads to Boot Camp Enrollment

After Grandpa died, and I was living with my Uncle Don and his wife, Ella, lots of changes occurred in my life, and it wasn't uncommon for me to hang out with a group of my friends at the Armory. The Armory was a tank division of the National Guard that housed two Army tanks. The man in charge of the Armory was Mr. Harvey. He was a kind man and he would let me and my friends climb on the tanks. He would also allow us to climb in and out of the escape hatch that was located on the bottom of the tank. On cold winter days, Mr. Harvey would let us guys play basketball inside the Armory.

When I sat in the seat of the Army tank, my imagination went wild. I envisioned all sorts of adventures. I got to know Mr. Harvey, who was also the head of the National Guard in Lexington. One day while we were playing basketball in the Armory, Mr. Harvey asked me to come sit in his office.

I walked in there with a little trepidation. I knew when boys were in high school in the United States that our country had a draft board. This meant that any male over the age of eighteen had an obligation to go into the armed forces.

I sat in a chair at the desk, opposite Mr. Harvey. He handed me a brochure describing how to fill your obligation to the armed services. The National Guard, however, had a new plan. If you joined the Guards before you were sixteen-and-a-half years old, all you had to do to fulfill your obligation was to go to boot camp for twelve weeks. After boot camp, you had to serve for two years in the local Guard. Then you'd be required to complete four years of inactive service before your obligation would be fulfilled.

Unfortunately, the Vietnam War was going on when I was in high school, and just the thought of having to commit to three years in the Army was scary. I went around town asking my buddies if they would join me that summer for the twelve-week requirement. It meant we would have to go to boot camp at Fort Leonard Wood, which was located in Missouri. Well, not one of the guys would go, so I went down to the Armory and signed up to go to boot camp for the summer.

I came home and told Uncle Don and Ella of my decision to go to boot camp, and it was a total shock to them. But they treated me like a grownup, knowing I'd be gone for twelve weeks in the summer.

***

During the next week at the end of the school year, I was scheduled to go to the train depot to catch a train to Kansas City. Uncle Don said he would like to take me to the train station. I was glad he wanted to participate in my life, and maybe this indicated that he supported my decision to serve in the military.

Uncle Don and I were sitting in the car after checking into the station because we had to wait for the train, and he said, "You do know that I went into the Army during World War II, right?"

I said, "Yes. I listened to the record that you left for Ella and Tim the day you were being shipped overseas to Iwo Jima. I also remember the stories you told about the piles of dead bodies stacked alongside the road. I think you said you were driving toward the service base with your assignment to work at the PX on the island."

"Yes," said Uncle Don. "But I want to advise you about three things when you get to boot camp. Number one: NEVER volunteer for any duties the Army offers you. Number two: Do NOT come home with a tattoo." He paused for a moment and then said, "Number three: Pay attention to your consumption of beer, because you can get addicted to drinking. These three things will keep you out of trouble."

I sat there in silence and was glad that uncle Don was concerned about me. No one had ever sat me down and given me their advice.

Twelve Weeks in Boot Camp at Fort Leonard Wood Army Base

Spending twelve weeks in Missouri with the heat and humidity was another adventure. Missouri had the same weather as they had over in Vietnam while the war was going on. All of us recruits got off the train in Kansas City and were put on a big bus that took us to Fort Leonard Wood. When we got off the bus, they had us line up in formation in our civies for our first lecture of what to expect during the first week.

Then the commander stated, "We need five volunteers to become firemen."

I started to think that if I was a fireman, I would get to learn how to put out fires and ride on a fire truck. That didn't seem like such a hard job, so I held up my hand. Then like a bad dream, I remembered Uncle Don warning me about not volunteering. Too late. I had already broken Uncle Don's first rule.

We were to have our first week of orientation and then seven weeks of boot camp. Some of my fellow recruits were older guys who were policemen from St. Louis, a fireman from Kansas City, and hillbillies from Kentucky. In our barracks, the men had a variety of backgrounds. As one of the first volunteers, they made me a fireman for my company.

This meant I had to stay around the barracks when I was on duty for twenty-four hours as a fireman, one day every two weeks. I had to get up early at 4:00 in the morning to start a fire using coal. It was the fuel for the boiler in each of the four barracks. My job was to have hot water ready for the troops in the morning before reveille. After the company went out on maneuvers, I would sit around all day reading, or I'd take a nap until the troops returned at the end of the day. I had to fire up the boilers again for the evening until 10 or 11 o'clock, at which time the troops were taking showers and shaving. The boiler water was heated by a coal burner, and the coal was piled up at the back of each of the barracks in the boiler room. So, I got to take it easy once every two weeks.

I learned many things while going through boot camp, but the most outstanding events in my mind were: learning how to drink 3/2 beer, how to fight gang-style with tips from Chicago hoodlums, and I was coached on how to get girls in high school by being cool with my actions and dressing the part.

I also became a loan expert because I saved my money for the end of the month. To help other guys out, I loaned them money for 100 percent of the cash amount. The guys from Chicago and St. Louis would spend their money the first week they got a leave, especially when our barracks passed inspections. But as I soon learned, making loans to other guys was not a secret on the base.

Sergeant Peters, who was in charge of my barracks, told the company commander that I was loaning money for 100 percent. After reporting me, Sergeant Peters came in the barracks where we were moving furniture. He singled me out and told me I was on KP duty for the next three weeks before I could go home. The new sergeant, who was a friend of Sgt. Peter's of my old squad had me cleaning and scrubbing the big pots and pans in the kitchen sink all day. I must have scrubbed 1,000 pots and pans in those two weeks. For sure, I was cussing under my breath at Sergeant Peters every day.

***

Another memorable experience occurred when I got to talk to an old Army sergeant who was a corporal and had already spent thirty years in the service. He had a bedroom at the back end of our barracks where he allowed me to sit and talk to him in the evenings. He told me he got his rank busted because he was on a mission of bringing an AWL person from one base to another for sentencing.

Sgt. Craig was his name. He was known to join other military policemen and get drunk in their hotel room while holding a prisoner.

Three of them would stay drunk for four days while on a stopover in Oklahoma waiting to catch another train to Fort Leonard Wood. The head military police supervisor reported that two solders were missing their deadline of returning the AWL solders. He had to go out to find the two guards with the prisoner. The three of them were AWL.

The supervisor who went out to start searching for Craig and his buddy was out over a week to get the AWL prisoners in handcuffs. The supervisor found the three passed out in their hotel room with no handcuffs in sight. The only thing visible were whiskey bottles. Sgt. Craig was stripped of his rank down to a corporal. Craig had a lot of stories to tell, but they were all based on drinking and survival in World War II.

Being a person who went through thirty years in service and combat situations, Sgt. Craig relied on alcohol to get rid of bad memories. This is why Uncle Don warned me about drinking and not getting addicted to it while in the military.

***

Before I left the base on my last day of duty, I mustered up the courage to find out where Sgt. Peter's barrack was located. Early that morning, knowing he would still be asleep because it was too soon for his new recruits to arrive, I took my footlocker lock and stood outside his door. I quietly closed the latch, which was on the outside of his door and placed my footlocker lock on his door, locking him inside. Then I quietly sauntered away.

Shortly thereafter, I got on the base bus which took me to the main gate where I boarded a scheduled Greyhound to Kansas City. I still hope he is in that room, because no one told me that I couldn't lend ten dollars for a weekend and then get twenty dollars at the end of the month after payday. I came back to Lexington richer and maybe smarter in experiences, but what I knew for sure was that I was in good shape to start football practice when I got home.

***

During my time in the armed forces, I experienced life with men who had very different personalities than I had ever been around before. I learned how to live a structured life, and I acquired knowledge and skills for taking care of myself in the real world. I never would have broadened my thinking and adapted as well if I had just lived my life alone in Lexington or Kansas City, especially at sixteen years old.

Chapter Fifteen
Getting Through Senior Year Was a Major Challenge

High school football practice started one week after I returned from boot camp. I went in the locker room to find coach Applebee to tell him I was going out for football and I wanted to be on his team.

Then once I had his attention, I said, "Coach, you really should find another student manager to help with the football storage room."

Couch said, "Go in the storage room and get your equipment. Then get out on the practice field with the rest of the boys."

Well, the first day after our conditioning session, which I did great at, I must say, all the other boys were puking and gasping for air. I was ready for the hitting. Coach lined me up as an outside linebacker on defense. Remember, I weighed about 150 with my gear on, and I was skinny as a stick.

Coach sent Dallas Dyer around my end so I went for Dallas pumping legs. When Dallas got around my corner, I laid out my body to hit this 195-pound All State fullback. Well, Dallas's knee came up and hit me in the chest. Then all I could feel was both Dallas and myself going down to the ground. I got the tackle but I couldn't breathe. I also couldn't see anything because my world went black.

Coach rolled me over onto my back. All I heard was Coach saying, "Brown, open your eyes!"

When I opened my eyes, Coach was fading in and out at the same time I was gasping for air, because I couldn't breathe. I knew I was dying, although I could see the sky, which was only a small blue circle. Other than that, all I saw was black.

I squeaked out, "Coach, I can't see."

Coach said, "Jimmy, let me turn your helmet around to where it should be. You're looking out your ear hole."

Then Coach Applebee's face filled my vision. I couldn't talk knowing at that moment that I was going to float up to heaven and never see Lexington ever again.

Coach grabbed my belt and yelled, "Jim, just lay still and start breathing through your nose."

I was thinking, *How can I breathe through my nose when I'm about to die?*

About one minute later, which felt like ten minutes, little gasps of air came out of my mouth. Then I could hear something Coach Applebee was saying to me.

"Jimmy, you are holding up my practice."

Then he turned towards Dave, the new student manager, and said, "Kid, keep holding Jimmy up by his belt and leave him lying down on the ground until he can breathe normally."

After gaining my life back, I sat up when the coach yelled over to the manager, "Kid, pick Jimmy up and walk him back to the dressing room."

After practice, Coach called me into his office and said, "Brown, I don't think you have the weight for this team. I really need you for our student manager, because the new kid doesn't know how to handle the practice balls and the routine we use around here."

So I stayed with the team who were the best in the state with no losses the whole football season. Only the last game of the season did McCook score six points on Lexington Minutemen who were undefeated. McCook used a trick play on the first play of the game after kickoff.

The coach pulled the team together on the sidelines and told them, "Guys, don't worry about the six points. Just play good ball."

The team went out on the field feeling hurt, but then came right back to score forty-seven points as well as keeping McCook from scoring again.

After football season was over, a lot of the Lexington players went to college on scholarships, but that is another story. Coach Applebee loved his team, but he was a tough, no-nonsense type of coach. He knew what talent I had, even if I did go to Army boot camp to get tough. He was my kind of leader, because I didn't want to screw up or he would have had my head for lunch. That's what happened to a couple of players who thought they could fool Coach Applebee.

The Transition from Football to Basketball

Everyone knew our football team was the best in the state, and they also knew our basketball team was the top in the league. I was happy to be chosen to travel to Lincoln with the team for our state final basketball tournament. I had bought my letter jacket, which was a big thing to me, because I had earned it by being the team manager for both the football and basketball teams during the last two years.

Around 10:00 a.m., all the players from the Lexington basketball team and I were sitting in the Coliseum watching the last team that was playing in the semi-finals that morning.

Monte Kiffin, who was nominated as best athlete in the state by all the coaches and sports writers in Nebraska, had been flown to Oklahoma and Norte Dame. He had received many offers from other colleges that wanted him to play football for their schools.

While sitting and watching the basketball game that morning, Monte stood up in front of the team, and said to the group, "Who wants to go with me to see Coach Jennings?"

No one answered. Then Monte pointed at one or two of the players, and asked, "How about you? Are you coming with me?"

Everyone he asked said no. They told him they weren't interested.

Then without warning, Monte grabbed me by my letter jacket and began pulling me out of my seat.

He commanded, "Brownie, you're going with me!"

I said, "Kiff, I don't want to see coach...who?"

He said, "Coach Jennings is the head coach for the Cornhuskers," as he pulled me with him down the hall to the coach's office.

I had never been inside such a big building, let alone going to see a big-time coach.

I said to Kiff, "Why do I want to see this coach?"

Kiff, still pulling me by the collar, opened a glass door that had the letters HEAD COACH underneath the name, Bill Jennings. We walked into a waiting room that had no secretary sitting at the reception desk because it was Saturday. Coach Bill Jennings, who was a tall man, came out of his office and told us to follow him inside.

Coach Jennings shook our hands and then said, "Take a seat, gentlemen."

He began talking to Kiff about how Kiff's team was doing in the basketball tournament. Then the conversation turned to other sports subjects. When Coach Jennings stood up and came around to the front of his desk, he looked first at me and then at Kiff.

"Who is your friend, Kiff?"

"Oh, this is Jim Brown."

Coach took the conversation from there and spoke directly to me.

"I see you have a letter jacket. How did you earn your letter? What position did you play?"

I said, "I was the student manager of the teams for the last two years."

Coach Jennings said, "Do you know how to tape ankles along with taking care of the boys?"

I said, "I took care of their gear and got to tape ankle wraps on players' ankles."

The next question from Coach was, "Are you planning to attend college after you graduate this year?"

I said, "I don't think I'll be going, but I'd like to go to college."

He said, "Have you thought about attending state college?"

I answered, "I wouldn't mind attending Kearney State which is close to Lexington, but I don't know what the cost would be to attend."

Coach said, "Would you like to go over to the training room to visit with Paul Schneider, the head trainer?"

Before I could answer that question, he had the phone in his hand and was dialing a number.

He spoke into the phone, saying, "Paul, I'm sending a guy, Jim Brown, over to see you. Could you take the time to show him your training room?" With a slight pause, Coach said, "He'll be right over."

Coach Jennings hung up and turned towards me saying, "Jimmy, go down the stairs that you came up to the second floor. Walk out the front door, then turn right, and follow the sidewalk past the columns until you get to the Coliseum. Then you will see a bright red door at the bottom of four stairs to your right. Walk through that door and ask anyone who's there where the training room is located. You want to go see Paul Schneider. Remember, his name is Paul."

Coach then stood up and came over to shake my hand. He said, "Jim, you go on over to the training room while I stay here to talk with Monte."

I walked over to the columns which had eight pillars in a specific area enclosed with black iron fencing. In a few more steps, the stadium was towering in front of me. I saw the red door, which I went through at the bottom of the four stairs. I ended up in a locker room with rows of lockers with benches in front of the lockers. I kept on walking towards the other end of the room. I came to a big open counter and there were a couple guys working on football gear. I asked where Paul could be found.

One of the guys told me, "Keep walking to the end of the lockers. The first door on the right is where you will find Paul Schneider."

I walked through to the next door on the right. Above the door was a sign—TRAINING ROOM. Standing in the room was this short man who was putting boxes on a padded table.

I asked, "Are you Paul?"

Looking at him, he had deep lines around the corners of his mouth which had a big smile. His face had a heavy stubbled beard, and a few long hairs were combed across his bald head. He stopped doing his task while standing there with a cigarette hanging out of his mouth. Smoke was rolling up the right side of his face and eye. He was wearing a gray T-shirt with the letters UN SPORTS across the front of the shirt. When he spoke, he had a deep gravel voice like he had been on a three-day drunk.

He looked at me and said, "So you're Jimmy Brown? Come with me. I want to show you the place."

He took me around the facility telling me as he showed me the in and outs of each room. He asked, "Do you know if Monte is coming to the university?"

I said, "I don't know, but I think Monte wants to come because all his buddies were thinking of coming here to play football."

Well, after the tour, I went back to the Coliseum to join the gang. The guys wanted to know where I went.

I said, "I went to see the training room and I met Paul Schneider."

None of them even knew what I was talking about and the subject was dropped.

Maybe a month later, Monte had signed on with the Cornhuskers. I received a letter from George Sullivan, Assistant Trainer, stating that he wanted me to come to fall camp with Monte Kiffin. I would be working with Paul and George in the athletic department at the University of Nebraska.

George told me to come to Lincoln with some of the students who had to take the entrance exam that summer. George then wrote that I would have to get my first year semester tuition and enough money for my first month of dorm rent, which was $150.00.

That summer I worked for the Stuckey's before going to Lincoln with Dick and Gary Neff to take the entrance exam. While in Lincoln, Dick, along with Gary, had been invited to a frat party because of Dick Stuckey's cousin, Harold, who was two years older. He had invited the Lexington boys to this big house where one of Harold's frat brothers was throwing a summer pool party. I was the hit of the party because I was showing the boys how to do single and double somersaults off their low diving board. The older boys of the frat house thought I would make a great member of their fraternity. This was the beginning of my experience in college.

Chapter Sixteen

Graduation Party in Denver

The summer after graduation from high school, I got the idea of having one last party. I decided it would be fun to go to Denver for a weekend because Monte Kiffin had to attend a recruiting meeting there with a coach, and of course, he wanted somebody to go with him. We rounded up three boys and two girls who would make the trip. We had two cars and we were totally excited to be driving to Denver. Most kids my age had never left the state of Nebraska, so this was a big deal.

We pooled our money and rented two rooms at a swanky hotel. The girls stayed in their room which was next to our room. The boys were riding with Monte Kiffin along with myself. The girls were Sally Lancaster, Ruth Snurr, and Luella Rupert, and they were riding with Dave Gilbert.

We drove about four and half hours from Lexington, Nebraska to Denver, Colorado and checked into our hotel around 4 o'clock that afternoon. That evening, we went to a restaurant next door and discussed what we were going to do on Friday for entertainment. We decided to go to Central City where they simulated an old gold town with costumes and old buildings.

The next day after drinking beer half the night, we had a hard time getting up to get ready for the day. We got to Central City around 1 o'clock in the afternoon and went to a bar that had an elevated stage. We sat at a front-row table, and then we ordered our lunch.

Up on the stage was a honky-tonk band and the musicians were in full costume. They played tunes and the audience could sing along with the band. Our group ordered three pitchers of beer to go along with our lunch. After our second round of pitchers of beer, we started singing along with the band. Every once in a while the band leader would stop to ask if anybody wanted to come up on stage and sing one of their favorite songs.

My gang started hollering, "JIM BROWN, JIM BROWN."

Then the boys picked me up and pushed me onto the stage. By this time I was feeling the beer. I went backstage and picked up a toilet seat, put it around my neck, and then stood up at the microphone and started singing **"Old McDonald had a farm."** As the group sang, when we came to an animal, I would make the sound of that animal and the crowd did the same. Pretty soon, I had the whole bar singing along with the band.

The band leader came over and grabbed me by the arm. I turned to him and took off the toilet seat hanging around my neck. Then I said, "Can you play one more song? 'Moon Over Miami?'"

As they started to play the song, I turned around, pulled down my pants, and showed the crowd the moon. I then turned around and pulled up my pants. I had the whole bar standing and cheering as I dove off the stage where my group was standing. They caught me before I hit the table. I slept all the way back to the hotel.

The second day, the gang spent most of the day around the pool sunbathing. One of the guests of the hotel was Darren McGavin who was in Denver for a play he was participating in as the main character. Some of the gang got to talking to Darren at poolside. Darren was interested in our football results as well as asking personal questions. He stated he was in Denver for only one week before he would get home.

The third day was Sunday and the gang had to take Monte Kiffin's car to get everyone home. Monte said, "I have a meeting at the University of Colorado for an interview. If you guys take my car, I will have to get a Greyhound."

Then Monte turned to me as the boys wanted to get back to Lexington and Monte wanted to get to his meeting.

Monte said, "Jimmy, will you wait here at the hotel and help me get back to Lexington?"

I said, "Maybe we can hitchhike home. So why don't you go ahead and let the boys take your car?"

I turned to the boys and said, "I'll get Monte back to Lexington when his meeting is over."

Someone from the university came and picked Monte up from the hotel for his 10 o'clock meeting. While I waited for Monte, I talked to the person at the front desk and told him about our situation.

The bell captain said, "There's a city bus that stops out front of the hotel." He then looked at the bus schedule and said, "The bus number is 872 and it will take you to the city limits where Freeway 76 is; that's where the bus turns around. Make sure to ask the bus driver for East 96th Street when you first get on the bus."

Monte was back at the hotel around 1 o'clock. We then went to the hotel's restaurant and had a hamburger. I told Monte about the plans to get us back home. We then picked up our suitcases and went out on the street to the bus stop. Sure enough, the 872 bus showed up twenty minutes later.

We climbed aboard and I asked the driver, "Does this bus go to East 96th Street?"

He said, "It sure does. I'll let you know when we get there. It's where I take my lunch break."

The bus ride took a long time and we had about four or five stops along the way. Monte and I were sitting in the seat behind the driver.

The driver turned to us and said, "This is where I turn around, but I have a thirty-minute lunch break."

I asked, "Is this where Highway 76 starts?"

The driver said, "Go to the corner, turn right, and then go over one block. That's where you'll see a sign for Interstate 76."

Monte and I stood up and grabbed our suitcases as we got off the bus. We walked one block and sure enough there was a sign—Interstate

76. I told Monte to follow me over the on-ramp to see if we could get a ride. As I got to the corner, I put my thumb out with Monte standing behind me. There were three or four cars that drove past us and didn't stop.

Monte said, "What are you doing?"

I said to Monte, "Turn around and start walking backwards. Then put your thumb out like I have mine."

Monte turned around and stuck his thumb out when the first car pulled over and stopped on the shoulder of the on-ramp. It was a little blue Volkswagen with whitewall tires on the small wheels. Because it was hot outside, the driver had both windows rolled down.

He asked, "Where you boys going?"

I said, "We're trying to get to Lexington, Nebraska before nightfall."

The driver said, "I'm driving to Holbrooke which is just past McCook turnoff. It's the best place for you to get off to get to Lexington. Climb in," he said.

Looking at the back seat, there was no way Monte would fit in that tiny back seat. Monte was six-foot-three and weighed around 220 pounds.

I turned to Monte, saying, "I can get in the back seat and then you can hand me the two suitcases. They can go in the back here with me."

Monte climbed into the passenger seat.

Then the driver said to Monte, "Buckle your seat belt or we can't go. That's a rule of mine."

Monte buckled his seat belt and the driver drove onto Interstate 76. He was a young man who was going home for his father's birthday as a surprise. We talked about our football season, along with other small talk. Then we took the road off of Interstate 76 to Highway 34, which was going east until we got close to McCook, Nebraska. The driver, Fred, pulled off the highway.

He said, "McCook is about half a mile down this road. I don't have the time to take you there. This is as far as I can take you."

I stood up in the back seat and opened Kiffin's door telling him to lean forward to let me scoot out.

When I got out, I said to Monte, "Turn around to the back seat and hand me those suitcases."

I grabbed the suitcases and put them down on the pavement. Because Monte was big, he turned to get to his feet on the ground and then he would stand up. But all of a sudden, there was a loud noise and there was Monte standing on the highway bent forward and not able to stand up straight. He was standing there with the Volkswagen seat belt still strapped to his butt.

I looked at the driver and his eyes were bigger then saucers, like he couldn't believe what he was seeing. I quickly grabbed a hold of the seat belt and told Monte to set back in the Volkswagen so I could get a hold of the buckle to loosen the seat belt. I then tried to slide the seat back into position, but it wouldn't go back onto the rails on the floor where the seat would normally go.

Fred, the driver, said, "I'll fix it when I get home."

I then wished him a safe trip back home. As he drove off, I'm sure he was cussing.

We started walking the half mile to downtown McCook. Of course, there were no cars coming by that could give us a ride. As we were walking, the clouds over in the west had turned from light blue to a dark gray. For sure a storm was coming our way. We were maybe three quarters of the way to our destination when the dark clouds hovered directly above us.

It started to sprinkle just as we approached a big Cottonwood tree.

"We could get under that tree before we get too wet," I told Monte.

Just as I said that, there was a bolt of lightning that stuck about a half mile from us. As I started running towards the tree, a loud clap of thunder startled me. I knew that standing under a tree was not the place to be in a thunder storm. As we stood there, we held our suitcases above our heads, but we still got drenched.

After standing there maybe five to eight minutes, a big semi-truck came rolling up to the other side of the highway. He pulled his airhorn and rolled down his window.

Hollering, he said, "You guys need to climb in my cab to get out of the rain."

So I grabbed Monte and pulled him across the highway. Getting around to the other side of the truck, we put our suitcases underneath the truck and climbed up in the cab with the truck driver. I was sitting in the middle and was starting to shiver when the truck driver turned his heater on to warm up the cab.

He said, "Standing under that tree was very dangerous because that was the tallest tree in the surrounding area."

We must have set there ten to fifteen minutes with small talk. The rain all of a sudden stopped and the driver said, "I'm not going into town. I'm on my way to Denver, but I hope you get into town soon."

We thanked him for caring enough to watch out for us. We climbed out of the truck and got our suitcases. Then we started walking into town, because we could see it from where we were. When we got into town, it was around 5 o'clock and Monte was getting hungry.

We found a filling station that had a little restaurant named Casey's attached to it. While we were ordering, I told Monte, "It's 5 o'clock, and we won't make it to Lexington before it gets too dark. And standing out on the highway, it might be a challenge to pick up a ride."

I then took out my little black address book and found the phone number for Dick Stuckey.

I dialed his number and when he answered, I said, "Monte and I are stuck in McCook. Can you come get us?"

Dick said, "Yes, but it might be more than an hour and half before I get to McCook."

I said, "We're on the main street of McCook in a filling station called Casey's. Thanks for coming to get us. See you soon."

Dick got to McCook about 7:30 p.m., and it was already dark outside. On the way home, I told Dick the story about the Volkswagen seat. Dick laughed all the way home.

Final Thoughts

As we come to the end of this second book, I wanted you to know I was happy to have graduated from high school. During my senior high years, I was in two class plays, and I contributed to getting the football team to the state champs. The basketball team went to the finals in Lincoln.

So back to the beginning, to all the men who told me, **"YOU'RE NEVER GOING TO AMOUNT TO ANYTHING"**...I just want to say, **"LOOK AT ME NOW."** I have an opportunity to go to the University of Nebraska where I will take on the adventure of college.

I ask you, "Did you ever turn down an opportunity when you graduated from high school?"

My college adventures will continue in Book 3 of the Jimmy Brown story. I hope you'll join me by reading my next book.

Don't miss out!

Visit the website below and you can sign up to receive emails whenever JAMES BROWN publishes a new book. There's no charge and no obligation.

https://books2read.com/r/B-A-QVCCB-SFFSC

BOOKS2READ

Connecting independent readers to independent writers.

About the Author

James Brown lives in Huntington Beach, California with his wife, Charlotte. He is a retired physical therapist who spent fifty-one years treating patients in his multiple offices and through contracts with rehab agencies for at-home patients. He and his wife have two grown sons, five grandsons, and one granddaughter. This is the second book in the three-book series about Jimmy Brown, the Orphan Boy.

Read more at https://jimmybrownclub.com.

www.ingramcontent.com/pod-product-compliance
Lightning Source LLC
Chambersburg PA
CBHW020548160726
47991CB00002B/633